LOUISA
LADY IN WAITING

Louisa
LADY IN WAITING

THE PERSONAL DIARIES AND ALBUMS
OF LOUISA, LADY IN WAITING
TO QUEEN VICTORIA
AND QUEEN ALEXANDRA

COMPILED AND EDITED BY
ELIZABETH LONGFORD

JONATHAN CAPE
THIRTY BEDFORD SQUARE LONDON

The author wishes to thank Valerie Pakenham
most warmly for her major work on the research
for this book. Many thanks are due also to
members of Louisa's family who have kindly
given invaluable information, especially
Sir John Balfour for his delightful reminiscences,
Angela Countess of Antrim, Alexander the present
Earl of Antrim, The Hon. Hector McDonnell,
The Hon. Honor Smith and Lady Rose Baring.

First published in Great Britain by Jonathan Cape Limited 1979
Albums and Diaries copyright © Roxby Press Limited 1979
Commentary copyright © Elizabeth Longford 1979

British Library Cataloguing in Publication Data
Antrim, Louisa, Countess of
Louisa, Lady in Waiting
1. Great Britain – Court and courtiers
2. Great Britain – History – Victoria, 1837-1901
I. Title II. Longford, Elizabeth Pakenham, Countess of
942.081'092'4   DA559.5
ISBN 0-224-01712-8

Made by Roxby Press Productions Limited
98 Clapham Common Northside London SW4 9SG
Researched by Valerie Pakenham
Edited by Carolyn Eardley
Designed by Ray Gautier
Production by Vanessa Charles
Typeset by Pierson LeVesley Limited
Reproduction by Essex Colour Services Limited
Printed and bound in Italy by Amilcare Pizzi s.p.a., Milan

Portraits of the Emperor and Empress of Germany on page 20 are
reproduced by permission of the Mansell Collection; postcard
commemorating the marriage of Prince Aribert and Princess
Marie Louise on page 21 is reproduced by permission of the
Radio Times Hulton Picture Library.

ONTENTS

INTRODUCTION

LADIES IN WAITING.
A CHILDHOOD AT
QUEEN VICTORIA'S COURT.

'I was much upset', wrote Queen Victoria when her beloved Lady in Waiting, Jane Marchioness of Ely, died. 'God knows what an awful loss she is to me.' The Queen went on to enumerate Jane's special gifts. 'She was absolutely devoted to me and we were so intimate. She was always so kind to all my children, and we looked upon her almost as one of ourselves.' Three months after Jane's death in June 1890 an invitation to fill the void at Court was extended to Louisa Countess of Antrim.

The entry in Queen Victoria's Journal quoted above shows what a Court lady at the top of her 'profession' could achieve: 'intimacy' with her sovereign and the royal family, so that she was 'almost' one of them. (Queen Victoria once explained to her eldest daughter Vicky that unfortunately a Queen could be completely intimate only with those of royal blood.) Of course Louisa Antrim had not seen the Queen's Journal. But she had many other opportunities of knowing about a Court lady's duties and how to succeed in them. Over a span of nearly twenty years' service to two Queens and their families, Louisa was also to become 'almost one of ourselves'.

At the time of Louisa's first waiting Queen Victoria was in her seventy-second year. She had long been known at home as 'The Widow at Windsor', abroad as 'The Grandmother of Europe'. A latter-day sunset glow had stolen across the scene since her Golden Jubilee of 1887, penetrating some of the gloom that she had decreed in memory of the Prince Consort, now dead for more than a quarter of a century. Visits from her numerous kith and kin helped to brighten up her palaces; though the very multiplicity of her royal relatives meant that there were always plenty of deaths among them to plunge the whole Court back into deepest mourning – unrelieved black, including jet jewellery. A young, fashion-conscious Maid of Honour who invested in heather-mixture tweeds for Balmoral was taking a calculated risk. It was a fifty-fifty chance that she would be in black cloth before the end of her period of waiting. The colour range of day and evening dresses for the whole Court was limited to black, white, grey, purple and mauve – but *not* the pretty pinky mauve that they found in fashion during one of the Queen's trips abroad.

In herself, the Queen was as forceful as ever, with a growing sense of responsibility for her mammoth Empire. Her experience was phenomenal. She knew exactly what should be done about every problem, and what would 'never do'. Attempts were made, for instance, to reduce the size of the multitudinous caravanserai that accompanied her every spring to the south of France. Could not the numbers of staff be got below a hundred? No. Her Majesty proved that every single one, down to the hundredth man or woman, was really necessary. Lame from rheumatism and her sight failing, she required to be driven around and read to even more assiduously than in the past. Since the death of Disraeli she had had no great favourite among statesmen, though her *bête noire* in the shape of Mr Gladstone still hung on. Her youngest daughter Princess Beatrice, her son-in-law Prince Henry of Battenberg and their young family who lived with her now filled her horizon, supported always by her faithful Household. With the demise of John Brown, the gillie, from erysipelas caused by drink and a chill, she turned instinctively to those other servants whom she herself had dreamt up and created, much as she had created John Brown – her Indians.

The hearty appetite of this little lady of under five feet tall had not diminished with the years. Preferred dishes were all sustaining: rich brown Windsor soup laced with wine, boiled chicken, mutton, haggis at Balmoral, potatoes, peas, strawberries and cream, pastries and puddings. A picnic tea at Balmoral would tempt her to try two of everything – scones, slices of toast, biscuits – after which she would say, sadly, 'I am afraid I must not have any more'. Her son King Edward VII was equally partial to a good tea of sandwiches, cakes and chocolate biscuits, between a satisfying luncheon and a splendid dinner. In an attempt to get her on to a lighter diet, Sir James Reid, her popular Court physician, recommended Benger's Food. She liked this milky cereal – but *added* it to the rest of her menu. She also accepted and ate any edible offerings, from home-made toffee-cakes to apples and *pomagne*. A fast eater, she never missed a course, helping herself to both hot *and* cold or iced puddings when there was a choice. But if the Queen never missed out on a dish, her guests frequently did. For the scarlet-coated footmen at Windsor and Osborne would whisk away all the plates as soon as H.M. had finished. 'Here, bring that back!' roared the hungry Lord Hartington on one of these occasions. The Queen had to smile.

Indeed the Queen often smiled in these mellower days. She was as likely to be amused as not amused, and particularly by ludicrous mishaps, as when a duchess dropped a bustle, if not a brick. A horsehair object resembling a large sausage was retrieved from the floor by a footman and handed to the duchess. 'I believe it belongs to your Grace.' Her Grace, denying it, ordered its removal, only to be told later by the footman that her maid had identified it as hers. 'The Queen burst into fits of laughter', recorded Marie Mallet, who became a Woman of the Bedchamber four years after Louisa Antrim.

As the Hon. Marie Adeane before she married Bernard Mallet, Marie had also been a Maid of Honour to Queen Victoria in the eighties. (The Maids were the juniors and of course single.) It is to her published letters that we owe the liveliest and sharpest picture of the late Victorian Court. Things were less strict by then than in the distant past. We happen to possess three separate commentaries on a Lady in Waiting's work, all written during the same four years at the beginning of Queen Victoria's reign. Between them they aptly suggest the spirit of a severe Court. In 1838 Lady Lyttelton was informed that while in waiting she must be 'an adviser, a woman of influence, a probable preserver or improver of the *national morals*'. Not being that sort of person, she laughingly described these duties as 'exactly *the very last* I could fill decently'. A year later the lady who was to wait upon Queen Victoria's mother was warned against the pitfalls: 'never to let your maid . . . say a single word to you about anything . . . within the palace walls'. Not only must she 'seal up' her maid's lips, but she should seal up her own as well, especially in regard to gossip about her fellow courtiers, 'because if once a prejudice gets into a royal head, it can never be got out again to the end of time'. Two years after that, a Maid of Honour was admonished about the need for 'the most rigid punctuality and obedience'. The least sign of '*ennui*' was incompatible with high breeding (no yawns, please, or nose-picking behind H.M.'s chair); 'you must accustom yourself rather to sit or stand for

Louisa's father, General Grey. Originally Private Secretary to Prince Albert, after the latter's death he became the Queen's first Private Secretary and served her until his own death in 1870.

Louisa's mother lived on as a widow in St. James's Palace in close touch with the Queen. She died in 1890, just after Louisa's appointment as Lady in Waiting.

The Greys' house in St. James's Palace.

The Norman Tower, Louisa's childhood home at Windsor Castle.

Louisa, aged four in 1859.

To dearest Papa Wishing him a very merry Christmas Louisa

Christmas card to her father from Louisa, aged seven.

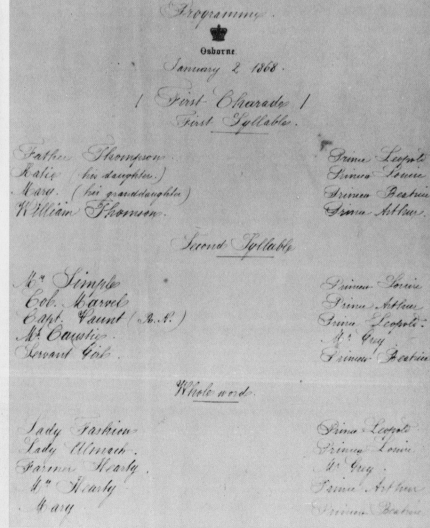

Charade at Osborne with Queen Victoria's children.

BUCKINGHAM PALACE.

23rd June, 1871.

FRIDAY.

OVERTURE, "Le Domino Noir," . . . . . Auber.

SELECTION, "Faust," . . . . Gounod.

ANDANTE, MINUET AND FINALE,
from Symphony in D, Haydn.

CHŒUR ET MARCHE DU BŒUF APIS,
"L'Enfant Prodigue," Auber.

GRAND SELECTION, "L'Etoile du Nord," : Meyerbeer.

OVERTURE, "Egmont," . . . . Beethoven.

MASQUERADE SCENE, "Le pré aux clercs," Hérold.

MARCH, "Athalie," . . . . Mendelssohn.

BALLET MUSIC, "Le Prophète," . . . . Meyerbeer.

Conductor, . . . Mr. W. G. CUSINS.

Louisa's first garden party at Buckingham Palace (she was sixteen).

Louisa and her sister Victoria dressed as shepherdesses
for a fancy-dress ball at Windsor.

General Grey fishing
at Balmoral.

Picture of King Charles's Window, Carisbrooke Castle,
made in sand by Princess Beatrice and given to Louisa when
they were children together at Osborne.

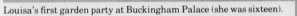

Osborne Cottage, where the Greys lived on the Isle of Wight.

General Grey with Prince Leopold, Queen Victoria's
youngest son (he suffered from haemophilia).

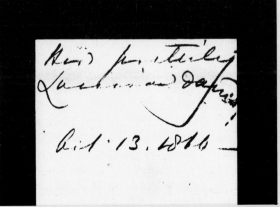

'How prettily Louisa danced' – a letter from Queen Victoria to
General Grey after the gillies' ball at Balmoral in 1866.

hours without any amusement save the resources of your own thoughts'. At the same time, 'your lips should be sealed' against all royal gossip. And to make sure of flawless discretion, all Ladies in Waiting were told not to keep a diary. Their pens must be as guarded as their lips.

Some fifty years later, when Lady Antrim, Lady Lytton and Lady Mallet were in waiting, we find a pronounced change in atmosphere, even though the tutelary goddess of the Court is still Discretion. Dulcie M. Ashdown, in her study of the subject (*Ladies in Waiting*) has ably summed up the new situation: 'The lady in waiting was now merely a companion to the Queen, a handsome appendage on State occasions, a confiding gossip in private, a subsidiary hostess to visitors and the penman of innumerable notes and memoranda on the Queen's behalf.'

Choosing a new courtier, however, whether male or female, was always a matter of regal headaches, whatever the conditions of employment. Sir Henry Ponsonby, the Queen's Private Secretary, was known to have exploded: 'Blow the Lords in Waiting. Every one I suggest to H.M. is objectionable. One has corns, another is dull, another is a bore.' Ladies could be dull also. 'Lady Southampton is most kind but her dullness is beyond description', complained Marie Adeane in 1880; 'she never originates a remark.' A questionnaire in four parts had been presented to Marie Adeane when she first became a Maid of Honour. 1. Did the candidate read and write French and German? 2. Could she play the piano and read music at sight, so as to play duets with Princess Beatrice? 3. Horseback-riding: what proficiency could she show? 4. Was she engaged to be married, or likely to be? Queen Victoria had a general objection to her courtiers of either sex marrying. Husbands, she believed, told all Court secrets to their wives; wives found their families a distraction from the royal service. Indeed, we shall see that Louisa Antrim sometimes found herself in difficulties over competing claims.

Louisa kept among the papers of her father, General Grey, a faded typewritten sheet of rules. On the back is written in her handwriting, 'Orders for Queen Victoria's Ladies in Waiting left in table drawer'. 'When the King and Queen receive Visitors at Windsor [this must have been redrafted in the reign of King Edward and Queen Alexandra] the Lady in Waiting is expected to look after them, see them in their rooms on arrival, be at breakfast and find out what they would like to do when not with Their Majesties. The Lady in Waiting is allowed a carriage in which she can take the Maids of Honour who have not a separate carriage for their own use. When the Queen does not require the Ladies' attendance at tea, this is prepared in the Lady in Waiting's Sitting Room for herself and the Maids of Honour who are expected to have it with her except under special circumstances. The Lady in Waiting is expected to act as Chaperone to the Maids of Honour and is responsible for them while in waiting. The Maids of Honour must not go out alone with the gentlemen or walk in the town by themselves.'

From these various words of advice and instruction certain general notions about waiting emerge. First, a tone-deaf Lady in Waiting was not much good. Music was the one art that the widowed Queen never banished from her palaces. If you were really musical, like Marie Mallet for example, you could influence the Queen. 'I am covered with glory', Marie crowed when H.M., at her suggestion, invited an operatic

star with a powerful voice to sing Wagner. H.M. loved it, instead of being 'blown out of her chair' as some feared. Sir Arthur Bigge (Lord Stamfordham), the Queen's Private Secretary after Ponsonby, was a musical enthusiast, having got his first post partly through his soulful rendering of 'The Lost Chord'. So was the Hon. Alick Yorke, Marie's uncle 'Nunks', whose duty was to wrestle with visiting *artistes* and whose pleasure to organize, produce and act in the royal theatricals. (The prompter's part was less important, since a claque of footmen was stationed at the back of the room with orders to burst into applause whenever anyone forgot his lines.) Maids of Honour, too, could forget their songs in the presence. The Queen, observing that one young singer had left out the tremolos, enquired of the girl's mother, 'Does she not shake?' 'Oh yes, Ma'am', was the reply, 'she is shaking all over.'

In the course of time, some of the Ladies' duties had been modified. There was more music and less dancing, though the Queen could still dance an old-fashioned quadrille 'with light and airy steps', as Ponsonby remarked. It was no longer necessary to be a good rider since the Queen did not go out riding, but to be good at 'jogging' was an advantage. Trotting beside Queen Victoria's pony-carriage in hilly Scotland at four miles an hour was a duty that had its advantages and disadvantages; at least one was warm while jogging. The cold at Balmoral was notorious. Only a few hardy characters like the Queen herself and Lady Lytton liked it. Lady Lytton slept well in her tiny bedroom and found the cold 'bracing'. When the Prime Minister, Lord Salisbury, paid a visit to Balmoral, his Private Secretary, the Hon. Schomberg McDonnell (Louisa's brother-in-law), wrote in advance that his room temperature must *not* fall below 60°.

Handwriting was another crucial matter. The Queen's memory harked back to the clarity of old Lord Palmerston's script. She could not bear a faint or inelegant scrawl. That the fault was now more often in her own bad eyesight than in her courtiers' bad writing, she would not admit. The vain efforts of Fritz Ponsonby, Assistant Secretary and son of Sir Henry, to make his letters more legible by concocting an ink out of black bootpolish are well known. Marie Mallet had a better idea. 'Can you send me a "Swan" quill pen?', she wrote in 1895 to her husband, who was private secretary to Arthur James Balfour; 'I hear they are only supplied to Cabinet Ministers so I thought you might "prig" one from A.J.B., especially as it will be O.H.M.S., for none of my pens write black enough to please the Queen and I want to make experiments.'

There was one Household tradition that nobody wished to see changed: the Queen's special relationship with each and every one of them. To be sure, they could not all be 'almost one of ourselves'. But the Queen's unfailing interest in their family affairs was genuine, not assumed. In return, the Household wrapped her in a warm blanket of sympathy. One condition of this sympathetic atmosphere at Court was that the Household did not indulge in too much mutual nit-picking. Marie Mallet, though somewhat critical by nature, realized that Lady Southampton was 'kind' as well as 'dull'; while Lady Lytton, despite her lacking 'the remotest sense of humour', was admirable and touching in her blind devotion to her children. The Hon. Harriet Phipps, the Queen's lady secretary, caused some friction in the Household through interfering, but was none the less 'very amiable'. Lady Ampthill was too inquisitive to be entirely discreet – 'we have to be a little bit on our guard' – nevertheless she had the merit of being 'affectionate'. As for Lady Antrim, 'I miss Louisa Antrim more than I can say', wrote Marie, lamenting that the lady she liked best was not at that moment in waiting, to help while away 'the many hours in one's room alone'.

It was on 22 September 1890 that Louisa received the invitation to become a Woman of the Bedchamber to Queen Victoria. The letter of invitation was signed by the Duchess of Buccleuch, Mistress of the Robes. In her diary Louisa described this exciting event in the most non-committal way, beginning her entry for the day with a customary reference to the weather (a habit, incidentally, shared by her Sovereign): 'Calm again – but dull & in the afternoon tremendous rain . . . I had a letter from the Duchess of Buccleuch proposing to submit my name to H.M. for l.in w.' Perhaps Louisa's own calm was due to a conviction that the glorious project would fail. The last line of that day's diary ran, 'but I fear Bill will never agree'. Bill was the Earl of Antrim, her husband; known to his family as Buzzard. He was a huge man and subject to inarticulate rages. Louisa must have telegraphed her refusal, for two days later came the diary entry, 'Telegram from the Duchess begging me to reconsider position very upsetting'.

Three days passed and Louisa herself had suffered 'A dreadful day of pros & cons brought about by a letter from the Dss. wh: makes refusal most difficult. I went to Church in the morning feeling rather sick all day.' Next day, a Monday, 'I was in a state of great indecision all day but letters & telegrams arrived & at last I wired acceptance to the Dss. – I trust it is well.' The Buzzard was away but Louisa had her sister-in-law Lady Evie McDonnell and her niece Lady Sybil Beauclerk for company. On the Tuesday she wrote, 'I felt sadly low & depressed – & made Evie & Sybil's life a misery to them'. But by 2 October the skies had cleared. 'Bill wrote agreeing to my acceptance of lady in waiting post, which is a great relief & eased my mind.' He returned home on the third – 'awfully kind'. The affair was clinched on 5 October. 'I had a most charming letter from the Queen herself', wrote Louisa in her diary, 'offering me to be lady in waiting – so I had to compose an answer wh. kept me busy.' Three days later Princess Beatrice welcomed her appointment most warmly. 'It will be a pleasure to see more of you again', she wrote, 'one likes to think of one of your dear Father's Children being about Mama.'

There was every reason why Her Majesty should be so eager to secure Louisa. She came of a family famous for its services to Queen and country. Her father was that General Charles Grey who had been appointed Prince Albert's Private Secretary in 1849 and, after the Prince's death, Queen Victoria's. Her grandfather was the Prime Minister Earl Grey of the Reform Bill. Through the Greys, Louisa was closely related to the Halifax family, to Lady Caroline Barrington, at one time governess to Queen Victoria's children, to the Ponsonbys, the Bulteels, the Revelstokes and the celebrated Earl of Durham ('Radical Jack') who had been Governor-General of Canada; as also, though on the wrong side of the blanket, to 'Bear' Ellice and Speaker

Brand who, as Louisa explained without fuss in her *Recollections*, were both descended from her grandfather Lord Grey's natural daughter by the inimitable Georgiana Duchess of Devonshire.

Louisa's youngest sister, Mary, was in turn to become Governess-General of Canada and afterwards Vicereine of India, through her marriage to the Earl of Minto, while Louisa's eldest sister, Sybil, had married the Duke of St. Albans. One of Sybil's grandchildren was to be Molly Duchess of Buccleuch. Louisa's brother Albert was to succeed Lord Minto as Governor-General of Canada.

On Louisa's maternal side there was beauty and prosperity but less social glamour. The much toasted Caroline Farquhar, her mother, was the lovely daughter of a banker, Sir Thomas Farquhar, who lived over his bank. After General Grey's death in 1870, his widow Caroline was allowed by the Queen to live on to the end of her days in St. James's Palace, the Greys' London home, where indeed Louisa Jane Grey had been born in 1855. Mrs Grey died peacefully in St. James's Palace just one month after Louisa received her 'charming' letter of appointment from the Queen. Thus in the very year that Louisa said goodbye to her mother's rooms in St. James's ('this dear old home') she was to forge her own links with the Queen.

We must distinguish three strains in Louisa's remarkable suitability for the job. First, Queen Victoria had a predilection for courtiers with a long 'pedigree' of royal service. They would already have the right ideas about loyalty and discretion, besides knowing something of what they were in for, through family memoirs and legends. Louisa, for instance, had a vivid understanding of the Queen as widow that dated from her earliest childhood. She remembered her sister, Mary, aged not quite four, at a royal children's tea-party, showing the Queen a locket of Prince Albert that her nurse had misguidedly hung around her neck. 'Look, there's P'ince Consort!' lisped Mary. 'The Queen burst into tears', wrote Louisa in horror, 'and hurried from the room.' This may have been the tea-party for which the six-year-old Princess Beatrice had personally written the invitation. It is an amusing imitation of the way her royal mama scribbled when in a hurry, and illustrates the story of 'Baby' Beatrice's favourite reply to unwelcome orders, 'I have no time, I must write letters'. There were plenty of stories about General Grey of which Louisa probably knew: how he 'would do nothing of the kind' when H.M. hoped he might tell a young Maid of Honour not to use so much make-up; and how H.M. sent a Lady in Waiting to warn him against taking too many tubs when he had his rheumatism – 'so much water cannot be good for anybody'.

Apart from the royal family's positive affection for the Greys (Queen Victoria confessed to 'a maternal feeling' for Louisa's sister Sybil, while Princess Louise described General Grey as 'a second father'), the Queen had always had pronounced negative reactions towards strangers. Lady Lytton recounted how embarrassing it was to bring someone new up to the Queen, knowing that H.M. would respond with 'a curious nervous laugh'.

Louisa's second strong card was her own perfect familiarity with all the sights and sounds of Windsor, Osborne and Balmoral. Up till 1891 they had simply aroused in her nostalgia for the past. Now they were to reappear as a fascinating present. Her childhood home at

Glenarm Castle, the Earl of Antrim's seat in Ireland. It had been Gothicized in the early nineteenth century, in what Lord Antrim affectionately called 'late Grotesque' style.

The Earl of Antrim and his youthful bride arrived at the family residence, Glenarm Castle, on Wednesday. The earl and countess, who had spent a portion of their honeymoon on the Continent, had lately been on a visit with the Duke of St. Albans, and arrived from England by the Larne and Stranraer route. They drove from Larne to Glenarm, a distance of eight miles, round the coast. At a short distance from Glenarm the horses were taken out of the carriage, and preceded by a band of Antrim artillery, and accompanied by an enthusiastic assemblage, they were drawn through the streets of the town, which were spanned in many places with triumphal arches, and afterwards to the castle, where his lordship briefly thanked the tenantry for their hearty reception. As he had told her ladyship, there was no welcome, he said, like an Irish welcome. There were great rejoicings throughout the day and a pyrotechnic display in the evening. In the course of a few days his lordship will be presented by his tenantry on the Antrim estates with an address, accompanied by a very valuable candelabra. The Countess of Antrim is daughter of the late General the Hon. Charles Grey, who was private secretary to the Queen, and she is niece to the present Earl Grey.

Group at Hambledon on the Thames, 1885. Louisa is third from the left at the back. Her husband was a champion oarsman.

Louisa's engagement to Lord Antrim in 1875. She met him at a houseparty in Scotland. Known by his family as the 'Buzzard', he was a highly eccentric Irish peer.

Feb^ry 19th

Marlborough House.
Pall Mall. S.W.

My dear Louisa

The Princess hopes you will bring your children to a little Party here to-morrow from 4 to 7.30.

Yrs affec ly

Charlotte Knollys

Invitation from Princess Alexandra to a children's party at Marlborough House.

Above: The Buzzard, in deerstalker. Unlike Louisa, he loved country life. Right: Louisa, with her first baby, Sybil, born 1876.

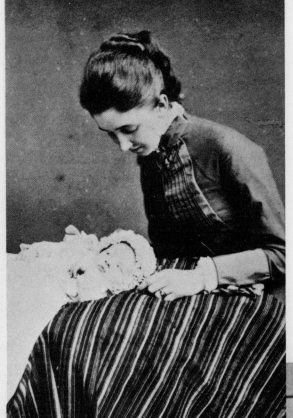

The Lord Chamberlain is commanded by THE QUEEN

to invite

The Countess of Antrim

to the Ceremony of the Marriage of

HER ROYAL HIGHNESS THE PRINCESS BEATRICE

with His Serene Highness

THE PRINCE HENRY MAURICE OF BATTENBERG,

in Whippingham Church, Isle of Wight,

on Thursday the 23rd of July, 1885, at ~~half past~~ one o'clock.

Gentlemen: Levee Dress.

Ladies —— Evening Dress. Demi-Toilette.

Invitation to Princess Beatrice's wedding. The Queen was at first much upset at her youngest daughter's engagement, but was soon won over by Prince Henry's charm and gaiety.

Dear Louisa,
I am so pleased
with that lovely little
seal you have so kindly
sent me. I have never
seen anything at all like
it, & think it so original.
Pray accept my warmest
thanks for it & your

Letter from Princess Beatrice thanking Louisa for her wedding present. The 'bee' monogram was designed by the Princess herself. Each of Queen Victoria's daughters had a special monogram.

Louisa on the steps at Glenarm with her son Ducie on her lap and Sybil, aged five. Her sister Mary Minto is behind.

Windsor had been the Norman Tower, her schoolroom once a state prison, with the names of Surrey, Edmund Fortescue and other captives carved on its stone walls. 'The public apartments', wrote Louisa long afterwards, 'faced our house, and we became good guides to the Van Dyck and Reubens rooms, the Waterloo Gallery and so on.' The Norman Tower's main wing stood in the garden that adorned the moat at the foot of the Round Tower. Log fires made the ancient rooms 'very comfortable'. The Long Corridor at Windsor held no terrors for Louisa in those days. It was a place for running races or playing 'Musical Chairs', with Princess Beatrice's French governess Mlle. Noreille, clad in lilac silk, to administer the forfeits: 'pique' (a stab in the back from her pointed finger), 'côte' (a blow with the side of her hand), 'raffle' (a merciless tickling).

At Osborne the young Greys shared the various holiday delights with the Queen's children. Louisa could remember her brother Albert helping Prince Arthur and Prince Leopold to build the model fort beside the Swiss Cottage, under the instruction of a professional engineer. And she just remembered, aged four, trying to make an arch with the Prince Consort for a country dance and afterwards falling asleep on her mother's velvet train. There was the royal swimming-bath, where Louisa 'revelled' in her daily swim – 'a ship with canvas walls anchored well out to sea. . . . Except for the jelly fish which came through the square holes in the floor, it was a perfect bathing place.' She had lively memories of skating, especially of opening her cloak to the wind and sailing across the pond like a galleon, or watching an unhappy female collide with the bank amid a flurry of scarlet knicker-bockers. One summer on the sea-shore, the Queen's grandson, Prince William of Prussia (the future Kaiser), aged six, lost his temper over some dispute and tried to kick General Grey, who caught him neatly by the leg, so that William toppled over backwards on the sand. 'Furious at this indignity, he seized my father's stick', narrated Louisa, 'and threw it into the sea. However, my father forced him to fetch it back and as I hope gave him a good tap with it afterwards.' Prince William, she also recollected, was desperately jealous of his aunt, Princess Beatrice, a child only two years older than himself. When 'Baby' Beatrice insisted once too often on his calling her 'Aunt', he shouted at her, 'Aunt Baby, then!'

'A little spitfire' was how Louisa saw herself as a child, with a high temper and high colour. The latter feature her grandmother Lady Farquhar disparaged as 'your brick dust cheeks'. Those cheeks, and her shining black hair, inclined Louisa to believe the Farquhar family tradition that they were descended from the Red Indian Princess Pocahontas. Louisa's young daughter Sybil remembered her mother looking tall and stately as Tennyson's 'Maud' (she was five foot eight), doe-eyed, walking like a deer, and possessing 'a beautiful little straight nose'.

As a full-blown Lady in Waiting in the 1890s, Louisa would not be subject to all the bizarre rules from which the Queen's ladies in an earlier age had suffered, and which Maids of Honour were still expected to obey. Susan Baring, Louisa's youthful kinswoman, was not allowed to invite even her own brother into her room. (Not that this can have been the worst of deprivations, since Susan's brother, the brilliant but eccentric Maurice Baring, would sometimes enter a room on all

fours.) The late Lady Ely, whom Louisa was in a sense replacing, had been too scared of the Queen's displeasure ever to see her son while she was in waiting. Marie Mallet, however, testified to the Queen's indulgence in these more liberated days. Ladies could now meet their families during waiting and easily get leave on special occasions. It was not mainly through fear of being cut off from her one daughter and two sons that had caused Louisa to write of agonizing 'pros and cons'. The great 'con' was the Buzzard.

Louisa and her sister Victoria first met Bill Antrim in Scotland, during a houseparty at Newton Don, the future home of Bill's sister Nina Balfour. Louisa was already a débutante of two seasons. On the occasion of her presentation at Court in 1873, Mrs Grey had given her a slim red leather notebook in which to enter each season's engagements. During her first season Louisa attended two balls and a concert at Buckingham Palace, a royal party at Frogmore, and one ball at Strawberry Hill and another at Apsley House for the Prince and Princess of Wales, quite apart from balls at the great London houses – Stafford House, Devonshire House, Londonderry House, Dorchester House. Bill's mother, the Dowager Countess of Antrim, had cautioned her son against 'falling in love with one of those Greys, who are just society girls and probably only think of amusing themselves'. Nevertheless Bill Antrim did fall in love with Louisa Grey and she with him. Her friend Elizabeth Home, at the Hirsel nearby, had carved a cabinet as a wedding present for the first of her contemporaries to marry. Louisa presciently popped a note into its top drawer: 'Keep this for me. Louisa Grey.' Proud owner of the cabinet, she married Lord Antrim on 1 June 1875 at St. James's, Piccadilly. Their children, whose family name was McDonnell, were all born in St. James's Palace, like Louisa herself: Lady Sybil McDonnell, 1876; the heir Lord Dunluce ('Ducie'), 1878; the Hon. Angus McDonnell, 1881. There was a monstrous Victorian riddle about Louisa and Ducie: 'Why isn't Lady Ann trim?' 'Because her heir is Dunluce.'

Glenarm, their ancestral home, was a Gothicized 'Castle' with four pepper-pot turrets on the coast of County Antrim in Ireland, thirty miles from Belfast. The boys would embark on the Larne-Stranraer steamer at the beginning of every 'half', for their English boarding school, Eton. Sybil, educated by governesses, cherished idyllic memories of Glenarm. 'The back of our big grey house . . . faces the sea and there is only a wall and a row of tall trees and the coast road between you and the beach.' The front of the house, with its imposing 'Gothic' porch and mullioned windows, faced south up a valley, the Glen, down which ran a small salmon river in 'little sparkling jumps', to flow by the Victorian battlements and barbican and under a stone bridge to the sea. There were fuchsia hedges beyond Louisa's garden, where she weeded, bedded out and thought nothing of digging up and replanting hundreds of bulbs in one day. It was always 'quite a relief to see green grass again – & to try to scrape off the London dirt'. We have a glimpse of the Buzzard on their sixteenth wedding anniversary, circling the estate on a tricycle. London seemed remote, momentarily less desirable, especially when Louisa heard there was an omnibus or rail strike; or that the public 'oddly enough' sympathized with the outrageous Sir William Cumming over what Queen Victoria called 'this dreadful "Card Scandal"' (the Baccarat case) in which the Prince of Wales was involved.

Bill's father had been a lusty, old-world type of aristocrat. He was marching his ten children up the gangway to the ferry when two sailors were heard in conversation:

'Yon fat man will not be far behind at meal-time.'

'Nor at bed-time neither.'

All the ten McDonnells excelled in vitality, with a preference for what was unconventional or even eccentric. Their group portrait has been hilariously drawn by Sir John ('Jock') Balfour, son of the vivacious Nina, youngest of the ten. Nicknames were rife. After Bill the Buzzard came the burly Mark, the Grimp; his wife was said to cheat at cards, to have been expelled from a ladies' club, and to blow her nose through her veil; they had no children, though their cook bore the Grimp a natural son. Alexander was the Fox, Schomberg was Pom; Evie was the Cloud, Mabel the Otter and her daughter Joan the Tiger. Louisa became the Oot. The Cloud kept house for Pom, a successful politician, Lord Salisbury's Private Secretary and later Minister of Works. As a young woman the Cloud had one day confided to her married sister the Otter, 'I dreamt last night that you and I ate Queen Victoria and divided the wishbone between us'. Later, having boarded the London train, the dream still haunted her and she said to her sister, 'I can't get the taste of Queen Victoria out of my mouth'. They soon had the carriage to themselves.

Jock Balfour heard stories of his uncle Buzzard's rages, occasionally provoked, alas, by Louisa's absences at Court. 'There is no doubt', writes Jock, 'that Buzzard felt lonely and resentful when parted from Louisa.'

In politics the Buzzard was as violent as elsewhere. During a referendum on Home Rule, he had the doors of Glenarm village hall locked, laid the key and a pistol on the table in front of him and offered to shoot anyone who voted the wrong way. 'Hands up for Home Rule!' Not a hand was raised. Fortunately Louisa was in entire agreement with her husband's views, if not his methods. Her Court diaries were rarely to venture on politics. When they did, it was nearly always to rebuke the Home Rulers. Queen Victoria would not have disapproved. Though she had warned Sir Henry Ponsonby, on taking office, not to be led astray by the politics of his radical wife, she saw no reason to warn Louisa against her bigoted husband. Their prejudices were hers. Louisa was terrified of him, as were his children, though not his grandchildren, with whom he was uniformly gentle. One evening, after a particularly long absence by Louisa, 'he suddenly pounded with his fists on a small sewing-table belonging to her . . . and, growling to himself, proceeded to smash it to bits and throw the bits on the fire'. On another evening, when she was at home and coming downstairs for dinner immaculately dressed, he hurled a cushion at her carefully arranged coiffure.

The 'civilized antithesis' of her husband, Louisa is remembered by her nephew for her perpetual smile, 'a fastidiously well-bred inflexion to her voice, her upright carriage (she was called 'Maypole' and 'Knitting Pin' as a débutante) and the atmosphere of 'discreet unruffled calm' that she radiated. Her accomplishments were entirely adapted to Court life. And this was her third advantage. Like the late Prince Consort, she would practise for hours on the organ, often in the Chapel

Royal, she was a painstaking water-colourist and good rider. Believing that upper-class mid-Victorian girls were virtually uneducated ('A little pianoforte playing, some desultory reading, French, German and Italian were considered more than enough'), Louisa kept a record in her diary of her now wide, if disorganized reading.

In her first year of waiting she ranged from Cardinal Newman's *Life & Letters* to *Miss Nobody of Nowhere*, from Kipling's *Light that Failed* to *Monica's Mischief*, from General (Salvation Army) Booth's *In Darkest England* to *A Born Coquette*, from *Our Mother Church* to *Mademoiselle Ixe*. Some of the books on her list she read aloud to her children; Scott and Shakespeare to the boys, Macaulay to Sybil. To do Lord Antrim justice, he too would read voraciously when not occupied with driving his cattle to market. (Not everyone approved of this latter activity. His agent once reported that some people thought it unseemly of him to drive his bullocks himself. 'A damned lie', roared the Buzzard. 'They were heifers!') An urgent telegram would reach his bookseller every so often: 'Books. Books. Books. Antrim.'

In her diaries (fat little brown cloth volumes) Louisa kept other lists besides her book list: the children's heights each year, the number of days spent in waiting (for 1891 '8 months 3 weeks & 4 days at Glenarm, 8 weeks in waiting'); the number of times she and Sybil took the Sacrament. Unlike Queen Victoria, Louisa went to Holy Communion every Sunday if possible, and one reason why she did not enjoy Balmoral as much as Windsor or Osborne was that the Anglican church was not near enough for her to attend it before breakfast. This aspect apart, Louisa's reactions to churchgoing were much the same as the Queen's. (Indeed there is still a Bible at Glenarm inscribed by Queen Victoria for Louisa's confirmation.) There was nothing Louisa liked more than a good short sermon. But extremes of length or gesture evoked pungent criticism in her diary. 'A clergyman from Belfast who told us for 40 minutes how we should forgive our enemies.' At Crathie Church, Balmoral, 'We had rather a terrible sermon from a man called Gordon who preached lengthily & tied his face into knots for prayer'. Finally, the end-papers of her diaries were a mine of worldly information. Published by Houghton & Gunn, 162 New Bond Street, London, they contained many advertisements of items essential to a Lady in Waiting: H & G's handpainted gauze fans from fifteen shillings, H & G's ten-guinea dressing bags in Morocco leather with silver and ivory fittings, H & G's 'Royal' Writing Cabinet measuring 14¾ inches by 13, equipped with everything from registered letters to telegraph forms. H & G told Louisa in 1891 that there was still a Penny Post in the UK, that parcels to Imperial India cost only one shilling, that income tax was sixpence in the pound and that a licence for a male servant or a carriage was fifteen shillings, for armorial bearings, one guinea.

As a child, Sybil once asked her mother why their family went on living in the Palace at St. James's after Grandfather had died. 'Because Grandfather wrote all the Queen's letters for many years for her', replied Louisa, 'and had been her most loyal and faithful servant.'

'Like Tuppen?' asked Sybil, referring to their butler.

'No, not exactly', said Louisa, 'though "Good Servant" is the highest title anyone can hold.'

Louisa herself was to hold it.

THE FIRST YEAR IN WAITING

WINDSOR, THE GERMAN
STATE VISIT.
OSBORNE AND BALMORAL.
1891

Louisa spent January and February at Glenarm, bracing herself for the challenge of a new life. It arrived on 10 March: 'Windsor Castle. At 3 Victoria [her sister] came with me to Paddington & saw me off with rather curling toes. . . . Dined with the Queen – quite a tiny party of ladies & we sat in her room afterwards.' How friendly seemed its bric-à-brac compared with the Corridor, where Her Majesty would normally sit after dinner. The Queen would drink coffee while the Household remained standing until she went to bed. Those suffering from corns or other ailments found this a particularly trying experience. Once, during a long 'stand', Louisa was to lean against the Queen's chair. She was tapped by the royal fan.

Next day Magdalen (Maggie) Ponsonby, Sir Henry's daughter, came early to see her, and Louisa went back with her for a happy reunion in the Norman Tower. There was to be much visiting between Towers and driving around Windsor Great Park. Old Mr Elmer, once General Grey's smart groom who had taken little Louisa out riding, was now gate-keeper in the Long Walk Lodge. The Long Walk . . . Louisa was now at the very beginning of her long walk with royalty.

Her first test came at a Buckingham Palace dinner – 'stiff & alarming'. But she enjoyed the visit to Windsor of the Dowager Empress of Germany (Vicky) and her daughter Princess Margaret (Mossy). After the Empress had unveiled a statue of Queen Victoria at Eton ('the boys very enthusiastic'), Louisa helped to receive the King of the Belgians, attended an Investiture and met the Archbishop of Canterbury and Mr Balfour at dinner. Lady Radnor wanted to see the prints in the Royal Library next morning; and that afternoon the Queen required Louisa's attendance on a drive with Princess Margaret. When she dined again with the Queen 'there was a band wh: was nice'. According to Ponsonby, H.M. was lucky ever to get a band; 'contracts' usually stood in the way.

On 9 May came another exciting letter from the Duchess of Buccleuch. It was Her Majesty's wish that Louisa should be the Lady in Waiting to the Empress of Germany during her husband the Kaiser's state visit in July. 'I have heard on all sides', added the Duchess, 'how popular you were at Windsor.' From 4 July onwards Louisa's diary could hardly find enough adjectives. The state dinners were 'enormous', the luncheons 'huge', the music 'beautiful', the military ride '*quite* lovely', the banquet in St. George's Hall 'splendid', the gold plate 'so gorgeous', the Albert Hall 'crammed & really imposing', the Guildhall 'a wonderful sight', the Palace Ball 'Bright & pretty'. There were only two drawbacks that Louisa ventured to mention: she and the Empress were always on the go, paying calls, visiting a naval exhibition and a governess's home, changing their dresses for the next event; and the Crystal Palace was a fiasco – 'we had an infirm parade of fire engines & a beastly dinner & most boring fire works – we only got home jaded at 1.30'.

This bad impression was obliterated during the last two days by a visit to Hatfield House. 'Such a dream the place is', sighed Louisa in ecstasies. After a 'magnificent' dinner in the Barons' Hall, the great Albani sang. For breakfast, Louisa conducted her Empress to the Barons' Hall, 'again beautifully arranged.' At 12 she rushed upstairs to change, when more guests began pouring in from London. 'Luncheon most beautifully done – everybody sitting down at 2.30.' They left by special train for Windsor, said goodbyes there, reached Paddington at 5.30, drove to Liverpool Street, 'where we took leave of the Empress. I got to Lowndes Sq. at 7.15, utterly dead beat'.

If exhaustion is well conveyed, the social tensions of the visit are omitted. The Kaiser had transferred his jealousy from 'Aunt Baby' to the Prince of Wales. Marie Mallet, who was with the Queen beforehand, noted how much the Court were 'dreading' what the Kaiser would say or do. (He responded well to his 'cordial welcome'.) The marriage of Princess Marie Louise and Prince Aribert was to end in disaster, despite an optimistic letter from Princess Christian, the bride's mother, to Louisa announcing the engagement: 'Louise is so happy'. Louisa's only comment was, 'I had to hurry out after breakfast to get shoes & gloves for the wedding'.

After a week for recovery Louisa continued her waiting at Osborne. This turned out to be twelve days' re-play of past idylls. One morning it would be 'our old walk to Osborne Cottage . . . all looking so like old times', followed by a drive to her former picnic place, Carisbrooke Castle – 'a lovely evening & Carisbrooke looked beautiful. . . .' Another morning she and Princess Beatrice would walk to the royal children's Swiss Cottage. With Maggie Ponsonby she revisited Albert Cottage – 'it looks so bright & pretty' – drove to Osborne Pier and rowed out to the swimming-bath 'where to my joy I had a bathe. I did enjoy it. So back in time for dressing & breakfast.' But she did not swim next day, believing like the Queen that one could have 'too much water'. 'I was afraid of bathing again too soon.'

There was many a 'delightful little cruise in the launch – in & out of the yachts'; and a visit from the Prince of Naples – 'a tiny man but nice . . . a large dinner'.

Three months of Glenarm, where the weather was often 'cold & blowy', prepared Louisa for the rigours of Balmoral in November. On All Saints' Day, Dr Cameron Lees preached 'such a beautiful sermon', having christened the Battenbergs' youngest child Prince Maurice the day before. Alas, the beautiful sermon was followed by a feast of 'poisonous turkey' which laid them all low. Among the guests was Princess May of Teck, being vetted as a suitable wife for Prince Eddy of Wales. One test was for her to be driven through the mountains in the Queen's four-horse carriage, getting out now and then with Louisa to admire an icy waterfall. A merrier note was struck by the Balmoral play, 'Cool as a Cucumber', and if the Queen went to bed early there were high jinks. 'Princess Beatrice played in the ballroom & we all danced a Russian Mazurka – & then kept it up wildly till 1.' Another resource was the game of 'willing'. The long 'stands', however, ended for Louisa in misery – 'so much pain coming on from piles'. After a laudanum prescription from Dr Reid she 'got through dinner wh: was something', but next day she was worse, though heroically struggling downstairs to dine with the Queen.

Still rather shaken, she joined the royal train for her first journey south with the Queen – '*most* comfortable, we had an excellent tea at Aberdeen – & a *sumptuous* dinner at Perth where we got out of the train for an hour'. Though the train was 'most beautifully driven & quite smooth', Louisa did not step out next morning, as the Queen was always observed to do, 'brisk as a bee'.

Louisa's appointment as Lady in Waiting to the Queen.

Windsor Castle. Louisa always preferred 'waiting' here, where she could be visited by her family and friends.

Queen Victoria in her sitting-room at Windsor. As she grew old her eyesight failed, and reading aloud was one of her ladies' duties.

The Long Walk at Windsor, where the Queen drove out in all weathers. She took a huge assortment of wraps, known to her ladies as 'the White Knight's paraphernalia'.

The Waterloo Chamber, Windsor Castle, where grand state banquets were held.

WINDSOR CASTLE.

—◆—

TUESDAY, MARCH 17TH.

1891.

THIS EVENING

HER MAJESTY'S SERVANTS WILL HAVE THE HONOUR
OF PERFORMING

A PAIR OF SPECTACLES

A Comedy in Three Acts, adapted from the French by
SYDNEY GRUNDY.

—o—

Mr. Benjamin Goldfinch	-	Mr. JOHN HARE
Uncle Gregory (his Brother)	-	Mr. CHARLES GROVES
Percy (his Son)	-	Mr. RUDGE HARDING
Dick (his Nephew)	-	Mr. SYDNEY BROUGH
Lorimer (his Friend)	-	Mr. C. DODSWORTH
Bartholomew (his Shoemaker)	-	Mr. JOHN BYRON
Joyce (his Butler)	-	Mr. R. CATHCART
Another Shoemaker	-	Mr. W. CATHCART
Mrs. Goldfinch	-	Miss KATE RORKE
Lucy Lorimer (Lorimer's Daughter)	-	Miss WEBSTER
Charlotte (a Parlour Maid)	-	Miss F. HUNTER

SCENE:
Mr. Goldfinch's Morning Room at Hampstead.

Stage Manager, - Mr. R. CATHCART.
Scenery Painted by Mr. W. HARFORD.

After which will be Acted,

A QUIET RUBBER

A Comedietta by
CHARLES F. COGHLAN.

—o—

Lord Kilclare	-	Mr. JOHN HARE
Charles (his Son)	-	Mr. GILBERT HARE
Mr. Sullivan	-	Mr. CHARLES GROVES
Mary (his Daughter)	-	Miss WEBSTER

SCENE — At Mr. Sullivan's.

——————

During the Evening the Orchestra, under the Direction of Mr. F. SCHÖNING,
will play the following Selection of Music:

1.	"AU SECOURS,"		W. Vandervell
2.	SELECTION,	"Boccaccio,"	F. v. Suppé
		(Arranged by F. Schöning.)	
3.	POT-POURRI,	"Musikalisches Action-Unternehman,"	A. Conradi
4.	SELECTION,	"The Gondoliers,"	Sir A. Sullivan

"GOD SAVE THE QUEEN."

—◆—

The Corridor at Windsor Castle, where the Queen sat after dinner. It was much disliked by the Court for its gloom and for the endless standing until the Queen retired. Only Lord Salisbury was allowed to sit.

Acting by Mr Hare's company at Windsor Castle, March 1891. The Queen wrote in her journal 'Mr Hare acts admirably . . . and is a gentleman as so many actors are these days'.

Victoria R.I.
Windsor Castle. March 17. 1891 —

Victoria (Dowager Empress Frederick of Germany) & Queen of Prussia

Windsor Castle. March. 18. 1891. —

Margaret Princess of Prussia. 1891.

Louise 18th March 1891.

Beatrice. March 21st 1891.

Henry of Battenberg March 21st 1891.

The guests for the state visit of the Emperor and Empress of Germany in 1891. The Kaiser, who loved ceremonial, arrived with a suite of nearly a hundred, and every corner of Windsor Castle was packed.

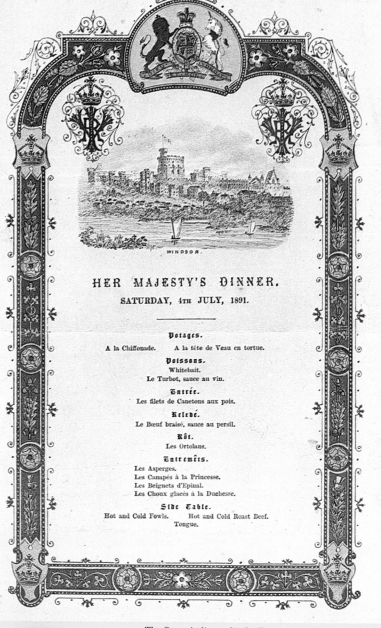

WINDSOR.

HER MAJESTY'S DINNER.

SATURDAY, 4TH JULY, 1891.

Potages.
A la Chiffonade.   A la tête de Veau en tortue.

Poissons.
Whitebait.
Le Turbot, sauce au vin.

Entrée.
Les filets de Canetons aux pois.

Relevé.
Le Bœuf braisé, sauce au persil.

Rôt.
Les Ortolans.

Entremets.
Les Asperges.
Les Canapés à la Princesse.
Les Beignets d'Epinal.
Les Choux glacés à la Duchesse.

Side Table.
Hot and Cold Fowls.   Hot and Cold Roast Beef.
Tongue.

The Queen's dinner for the Emperor and Empress of Germany on the first day of their state visit.

WINDSOR CASTLE

SATURDAY EVENING, 4TH JULY, 1891.

OVERTURE, "*Rienzi,*" . . . . Wagner.

SELECTION, "*Carmen,*" . . . Bizet.

DIVERTISSEMENT, "*Cinq Mars,*"

Gounod.

MARCHE INDIENNE, "*L'Africaine,*"

Meyerbeer.

POLNISCHE TÄNZE, . . . Emil Bach.

OVERTURE, "*Le Cheval de Bronze,*"

Auber.

CONDUCTOR, . . Mr. W. G. Cusins.

Music at the Queen's dinner for the German Emperor.

The Empress. Louisa was in waiting to her for the visit.

The Kaiser, Queen Victoria's 'difficult' grandson, Willy.

The Lord Chamberlain *is commanded by*
THE QUEEN

to invite _____

The Countess of Antrim
to the Ceremony of the Marriage of
HER HIGHNESS THE PRINCESS LOUISE OF SCHLESWIG-HOLSTEIN
with His Highness
THE PRINCE ARIBERT OF ANHALT,
in St *George's Chapel, Windsor Castle,*
on Monday, the 6th of July, 1891, at 4 o'clock.

Gentlemen. Levée Dress.
Ladies. ___ Evening Dress. Demi-Toilette.

PRINCE ARIBERT OF ANHALT-DESSAU AND PRINCESS LOUISE OF SCHLESWIG-HOLSTEIN

'Louise is so happy – it does one good to see her beaming face,' wrote the bride's mother; but this marriage turned out badly. Prince Aribert tried to divorce his wife in 1900 after 'squandering her dowry'. Queen Victoria sent a firm telegram: 'Tell my granddaughter to come home to me. VR.'

RECEPTION BY THE CORPORATION OF THE CITY OF LONDON.
of
His Imperial Majesty The German Emperor.
at the Guildhall on Friday July the 10th 1891.
The Rt Hon. JOSEPH SAVORY, Lord Mayor.

WILLIAM FARMER ESQ. | SHERIFFS.
AUGUSTUS H. G. HARRIS ESQ. |

ADMIT *The Countess of Antrim.*

No 652
NOT TRANSFERABLE.

WILLIAM H. WILLIAMSON ESQ.
Chairman of the Committee.

Designed & Printed by Blades, East & Blades, 23 Abchurch Lane, London.

Reception at the Guildhall by the Lord Mayor of London for the Emperor and Empress.
'v. enthusiastic & crammed with guests,' wrote Louisa.

INSTRUCTIONS FOR COACHMEN.

Visit of H.I.M. The German Emperor
To GUILDHALL, 10TH JULY, 1891.

After setting down drive round and rank at once on the

NORTH SIDE OF CHEAPSIDE,
AS DIRECTED BY THE POLICE.

HENRY SMITH,
CITY POLICE OFFICE,   LT.-COLONEL,
July, 1891.   *Commissioner of Police.*

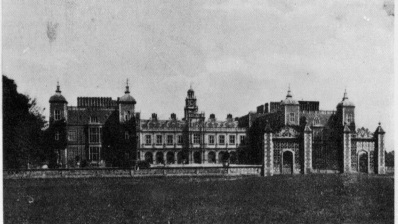

LIST OF VISITORS TO HATFIELD HOUSE.

(11TH, 12TH, AND 13TH JULY, 1891.)

ALPHABETICALLY ARRANGED.

Alderson, General Sir Henry	Temperance Hotel.
Alderson, Lady	West Wing: Housekeeper's Room.
Alderson, Miss	East Wing: Nursery Kitchen.
Antrim, Countess of	„ „ Fir Room.
Arran, Earl of	Mr. Ashton's.
Balfour, Right Honourable Arthur	Gate House: First Floor, No. 6.
Barrington, Honourable Eric	„ „ Attic, No. 1.
Bieberstein, Secretary of State, Freiherr Marschall von	East Wing: Queen Anne's Room.
Brockdorff, Ober Hofmeisterin Grafin von	East Wing: Myrtle Room.
Buccleuch, Duke and Duchess of	West Wing: Lime Room and Dressing Room.
Cambridge, Duke of	East Wing: King James' Bed Room.
Chancellor, the Lord, and Lady Halsbury	West Wing: Hornbeam Room and Dressing Room.
Cecil, Lord and Lady Robert	St. Audrey's.
Cecil, Lady Gwendolen	East Wing: Blue Dressing Room.
Cecil, Lord Edward	Gate House: Ground Floor, No. 2.
Cecil, Lord Hugh	Tennis Court.
Cecil, Lord and Lady Eustace	East Wing: Pine Room and Bath Room.
Clanwilliam, Admiral, Earl of, and Countess of	West Wing: Beech and Hazel
Clarence and Avondale, Duke of	W
Colville, Lord	M
Commerell, Admiral, Sir Edmund	Ga
Cranborne, Viscountess	E
Cranborne, Viscount	Ga
Currie, Sir Philip	M
De Ros, General Lord	Ga

The Kaiser's state visit to Hatfield, home of the Prime Minister, Lord Salisbury. Fitting in the guests was a problem here, as at Windsor. Some of Lord Salisbury's family had to be boarded out in gate lodges.

'Carisbrooke looked beautiful & we clambered all over it.' Louisa spent her first 'waiting' at Osborne revisiting childhood haunts.

Osborne on the Isle of Wight was designed by Prince Albert and was full of his memories for the Queen.

Whippingham Church, near Osborne.

The terrace at Osborne, where music was played
on summer evenings.

Her Majesty's Dinner.

OSBORNE

HER MAJESTY'S DINNER.

FRIDAY, 24th JULY, 1891.

Potages.
Cock-a-leekie.   La Crême d'Orges.

Poissons.
Whitebait.
Les filets de Soles à la Marechàle.

Entree.
Les Croquettes à la Milanaise.

Relèves.
Haunch of Venison.
Roast Beef.

Rot.
Les Cailles.

Entremets.
Les Pois sautés au beurre.
Kresse Brodchen.
Les petits Savarins au Curaçoa.
Les Meringues à la Vanille.

Side Table.
Hot and Cold Fowls.   Tongue.   Cold Beef.

The Queen's dinner for the young Prince of Naples. 'A tiny
man but nice', wrote Louisa. 'A fine head . . . but
dreadfully short', wrote the Queen.

Lady Salisbury on a visit to Osborne with her husband.
She and the Queen much admired and liked each other.

Band of the   Portsmouth
Royal Marines,   Division.

Programme of Music.

Herzogin-Connaught Marsch.

1	Ständchen	..	Schubert.
2	Overture	"Ruy Blas"	Mendelssohn.
3	Andante from the C Minor Symphony		Beethoven.
4	Kamarinskaja (Fantasia on Russian Volkslieder)		Glinka.
5	Selection	"Tannhäuser" (INCLUDING SONG TO THE EVENING STAR)	Wagner.
6	Marsch	"Geburtstag"	Gutterjahn.

God Save the Queen.

25TH JULY. 1891.   GEORGE MILLER, Bandmaster.

Programme of music by the Queen's favourite Royal Marine Band.

Balmoral, the Queen's 'Highland Palace' and favourite home. It was much dreaded by the Court for its cold, boredom and discomfort. Louisa fell ill on her first visit. (Above) the Hall at Balmoral, hung with stags shot by Prince Albert.

9th Nov., 1891.

Amateur theatricals at Balmoral were much enjoyed by the Queen.

The drawing-room at Balmoral. The whole house was decorated in royal tartans.

Louisa's first train journey with the Queen from Balmoral. The Queen always emerged full of energy at Windsor, but her ladies found it exhausting.

LONDON AND NORTH WESTERN RAILWAY.

ARRANGEMENT OF CARRIAGES

COMPOSING

HER MAJESTY'S TRAIN,

FROM BALLATER TO WINDSOR,

ON FRIDAY, THE 20TH, AND SATURDAY, THE 21ST NOVEMBER, 1891.

Engine.	Break.	For Men Servants.	For Pages and Upper Servants.	Dressers and Ladies' Maids.	Countess of Antrim. The Hon. Ethel Cadogan. Miss McNeill. Miss Bauer. Miss Cochrane.	Children of Prince and Princess Henry of Battenberg and Attendants.	Queen's Dressers.	Her Majesty AND Princess Beatrice.	Personal Servants.	Prince Henry of Battenberg.	Sir John McNeill. Sir Fleetwood Edwards. Major Walter. Dr. Reid. Mr. Muther.	The Munshi Abdul Kerim. Indian Attendants.	Directors.	Directors.	Queen's Fourgon.	Break.
	Van. No. 210.	Sleeping Carriage. No. 870.	Day Saloon. No. 72.	Day Saloon. No. 85.	DOUBLE SALOON. No. 131.	DOUBLE SALOON. No. 1.		Royal Saloons.		Family Saloon. No. 132.	Double Saloon. No. 153.	Double Saloon. No. 71.	Double Saloon. No. 4.	Lavatory Compo. No. 999.	Carriage Truck. No. 137.	Van. No. 272.

< — 258 feet 6 inches — > < — 274 feet 6 inches — >

McCORQUODALE & Co., LIMITED, Cardington Street, London, N.W.

Sir Henry Ponsonby, the Queen's Secretary, and Mr Muther, her Librarian.

The Queen's Own Highland Guard on parade for her departure from Ballater, the local station for Balmoral.

MENU.

Consommé.   Scotch Broth.

Turbot—Lobster Sauce.
Fried Fillets of Sole.

Mutton Cutlets.   Braised Fillet of Beef.

Roast Chicken.
Pheasant.   Partridge.

Savarin Pudding.
Madeira Jelly.   Stewed Pears.
Pastry.

Dessert.

*Station Hotel,
Perth, 20th November, 1891.*

London Art Printer, Perth.

'Sumptuous dinner' at Perth Station, the first stop on the way south.

SETTLING IN

OSBORNE AND BALMORAL.
CAMPAIGNING AT GLENARM.
TO COBURG WITH THE QUEEN.
DEATH OF PRINCE HENRY.
1892-1896

During the next period of five years Louisa emerged as the most sympathetic of Court ladies. Her sympathies were much in demand when, in January 1892, the royal family were prostrated by a sudden tragedy. A month after the engagement of Prince Eddy and Princess May, the Prince died from complications following influenza – that 'atrocious' and 'vicious disease', as Louisa called it. To those in the know, Queen Victoria's touching tribute to her grandson – 'full of promise for the future' – had an ironic ring. Promise of what? More scrapes? There was unconscious irony also in Louisa's description of Princess May's mourning dress at Osborne: 'She looked very pretty in her dress, black, and white cuffs & collar.' Poor Eddy's amiable weakness had been nailed in the nickname, 'Collars and Cuffs'.

This waiting at Osborne was an agony of gloom. When the Princess of Wales arrived, 'she kissed us all – a little catch in her throat gave me such an ache', wrote Louisa. The Queen's drawing-room after dinner was so 'awful', that on the next occasion Louisa and Rosa Hood were the only ladies to venture in, 'wh: terrified us'. Louisa's brother-in-law, Pom McDonnell, cheered her up by taking her to see Oscar Wilde's play *An Ideal Husband*, which she found 'really very good but cynical'. Cynicism apart, Prince George of Wales, Eddy's brother, was clearly the 'ideal husband' for the bereaved Princess May. They were married next year.

Meanwhile life became normal again at Windsor, where Louisa indulged in her former pursuits of organ lessons – 'I do get on a *little*' – and riding. 'A lovely morning & at 8.15 I went off with Maggie for a ride on a nice quiet beast called Kassassin – I *did* enjoy myself & never thought I should ride here again.'

The General Election, however, was depressing. 'A bad day at elections', she wrote. 'Old Gladstone got a real start now – though he lost 4000 votes in Midlothian. A nasty day, cold & disagreeable.' And more disagreeable still when 'Old Gladstone' and his Home Rule policy for Ireland were found to have won. 'Lord Salisbury went to Osborne to resign, alas!' Three weeks later she wrote bitterly: 'Mr Gladstone knocked down by a heifer – another old gentleman of 83 would have succumbed – of course he is none the worse.' But Louisa was consoled next year, when Mr Balfour visited Belfast in April and received a hero's welcome; not least at Glenarm where he stayed, as did Lord Salisbury next month. Louisa's account of the triumph was sent to H.M. via Harriet Phipps, and appears in Queen Victoria's published *Letters*. A mock-up of Gladstone's Home Rule Bill was torn to shreds, burnt and stamped underfoot: 'I could not help longing for Mr Gladstone to be present. . . .' Mr Balfour declared to a vast crowd that 'tyrannical majorities' in the Commons were as bad as, if not worse than, tyrannical monarchs, and should be treated accordingly. With this encouragement, the House of Lords, wrote Louisa jubilantly, 'kicked out the Home Rule Bill 419 to 41!' Even Balmoral on a snowy November night could be dealt with: '. . . the servants' dance, for an hour . . . I danced myself red-hot.'

Louisa was now to experience really stiff festivities, very different from the whisky-wild gillies' ball at home. In April 1894 she was Acting Mistress of the Robes to the Queen at the Coburg wedding. It was thronged with royalties – 'never saw so many', wrote Sir Henry Ponsonby. Queen Victoria's granddaughter Princess 'Ducky' of Edinburgh (and Coburg) was marrying the Queen's grandson 'Ernie' of Hesse. On her arrival, Louisa's maid Bodley 'broke down & had one of her worst headaches – but Minnie [Cochrane]'s maid helped me'. This was as well, since ill-attired ladies were not welcome at the rigid Coburg court, despite its ruler being an Englishman, Queen Victoria's son Alfred. Louisa was 'glad not to live there'.

Nor were the fashions prepossessing: high, stiffened necks, cumbrous capes over hideously puffed sleeves, flat hats from which the piled-up harvest seemed about to slide off, scraped back hair and fuzzy fringes; only the narrow waists looked feminine. Sir Henry Ponsonby complained of 'all day dressing and bothering'.

Of the wedding itself, Louisa wrote: 'Luckily fine till the evening when a heavy thunderstorm . . . came on. At 11.30 we all assembled at the Schloss & the marriage took place at 12.30, very pretty it was.' The bride's sister-in-law, Princess 'Alicky' of Hesse, chose this moment to announce her engagement to 'Nicky', the young Tsarevitch. 'I was thunderstruck', wrote Queen Victoria. If John Brown had been alive, with his second sight, he would have taken the 'heavy thunderstorm' to portend the break-up of both marriages: the Coburgs' by divorce, the Russians' by murder.

The year 1895 brought Court changes, some of them pleasing to Louisa. Fritz Ponsonby arrived and Marie Mallet returned. Marie noticed that nothing had changed at Balmoral since she left five years before: 'same plum cake, even the number of biscuits on the plate . . . absolutely identical'. Only some of the old faces were gone, Sir Henry's being one, and a selection of new dogs followed H.M.'s pony-chair.

The most startling change in the Household was caused by the sudden engagement of a Maid of Honour, Ina McNeill, to a widower, Princess Louise's father-in-law, the Duke of Argyll. No one dared tell the Queen. The Duke at last confessed, and Louisa wrote, ' . . . so now the strain will I hope be over'.

A highlight of the year – if one could call it that – was the visit of the King of Portugal. Marie commented bitingly on his greed, but Louisa merely noted (thankfully?) that his visit to Mass on Sunday 'took all the morning', and he 'left at cockcrow' next day. She herself departed from Balmoral on the Friday, 'with intense satisfaction'.

The real highlight of 1895 was Louisa's discovery of bicycling. Everybody was doing it. Marie practised on the Windsor 'Slopes'. The Otter, Louisa's sister-in-law, bicycled about Cumberland on her County Council business, carrying a spare dress to change behind a hedge. Louisa herself tended to get 'red-hot' at first. But soon all places she visited were judged by their bikeability. At Saighton, 'I tried to bike a little', at Viceregal Lodge, Dublin, 'the paths are wonderful for it . . . I biked & got on very well'. She and Sybil bought two 'real beauties' for Glenarm. In the Bois de Boulogne Louisa hired a bicycle '& had a most heavenly spin'.

A terrible new affliction smote the Royal Family in January 1896, when Prince Henry ('Liko') of Battenberg died from fever caught during the Ashanti war. This blow was to darken the Queen's last years. The day before a mourning card from Princess Beatrice arrived, Louisa had written in her diary, 'Windsor. March 1. Dinner dull & silent'. It seemed like the death of Prince Eddy all over again.

Prince Eddy, eldest son of the Prince of Wales. His death in January 1892, just before the day appointed for his marriage to Princess May of Teck, had plunged Osborne into gloom by the time Louisa returned there. 'We went into the Queen's drawing-room after dinner,' she wrote on 3 February, 'which was quite awful.'

Princess Alexandra, Prince Eddy's mother. 'She kissed us all – a little catch in her throat gave me such an ache', wrote Louisa.

OSBORNE,

January 26th, 1892.

I must once again give expression to my deep sense of the loyalty and affectionate sympathy evinced by my subjects in every part of my Empire on an occasion more sad and tragical than any but one which has befallen me and mine, as well as the Nation. The overwhelming misfortune of my dearly loved Grandson having been thus suddenly cut off in the flower of his age, full of promise for the future, amiable and gentle, and endearing himself to all, renders it hard for his sorely stricken Parents, his dear young Bride, and his fond Grandmother to bow in submission to the inscrutable decrees of Providence.

The sympathy of millions, which has been so touchingly and visibly expressed, is deeply gratifying at such a time, and I wish, both in my own name and that of my children, to express, from my heart, my warm gratitude to *all*.

These testimonies of sympathy with us, and appreciation of my dear Grandson, whom I loved as a Son, and whose devotion to me was as great as that of a Son, will be a help and consolation to me and mine in our affliction.

My bereavements during the last thirty years of my reign have indeed been heavy. Though the labours, anxieties, and responsibilities inseparable from my position have been great, yet it is my earnest prayer that God may continue to give me health and strength to work for the good and happiness of my dear Country and Empire while life lasts.

VICTORIA, R.I.

The Queen's message to the nation after Prince Eddy's death.

Despite her grief, Queen Victoria had had serious doubts about Prince Eddy's 'steadiness'.

Acting at Balmoral, Autumn 1892. 'A nice diversion', wrote Louisa.

'Count Gleichen's answer to my invitation to ride, inferring
a previous engagement' (with Princess Beatrice).

BALMORAL.

A Fair Encounter

a comedietta
in one act

Lady Clara St. John .. Hon. Mary Hughes

Mrs Celia Grenville .. Hon. Ethel Cadogan

scene - Lady Clara's boudoir

Drawing-room comedy performed
by the Maids of Honour.

St. John Ambulance Association,

BEING THE AMBULANCE DEPARTMENT OF
The Grand Priory of the Order of the Hospital of St. John of Jerusalem in England.

President:
HIS ROYAL HIGHNESS THE PRINCE OF WALES, K.G.
(Grand Prior of the Order.)

Director of the Ambulance Department, and Chairman of Committee.
THE RIGHT HON. THE EARL OF LIMERICK, K.P.

Deputy Chairman.
SIR VINCENT B. KENNETT-BARRINGTON, M.A., LL.M.

Chief Secretary.
LIEUT.-COLONEL SIR HERBERT C. PERROTT, BART.

Assistant Secretary and Storekeeper.
GEORGE B. TURNBULL, ESQ.

This is to certify that *Louise Countess Antrim*
who obtained an Elementary Certificate of ability to render "First Aid to the Injured," has attended a
course of Instruction in Nursing at the *Deeside* Centre of the
St. John Ambulance Association, and has been successful in passing the Examination.

Beatrice
President of Centre.

Surgeon Instructor.

Surgeon Examiner.

Local Hon. Secretary.

ST. JOHN'S GATE, CLERKENWELL,
LONDON, E.C. *Novr* 1892.

Nursing certificate awarded by Princess Beatrice.
Lectures helped to pass the time at Balmoral.

A. W. James Balfour

The fight against Gladstone's Home Rule Bill, April 1893. A.J. Balfour on his campaign visit to Belfast found Louisa an ardent ally. 'I could not resist letting the Queen know of its success', she wrote to Harriet Phipps, the Queen's lady secretary. 'The Bill was burnt . . . and stamped on amidst wild enthusiasm.'

ULSTER AND THE UNION.

—·—

IMMENSE DEMONSTRATION IN BELFAST.

ENTHUSIASTIC RECEPTION OF MR. BALFOUR.

—·—

The carriage arriving at Glenarm for Lord Salisbury's visit.

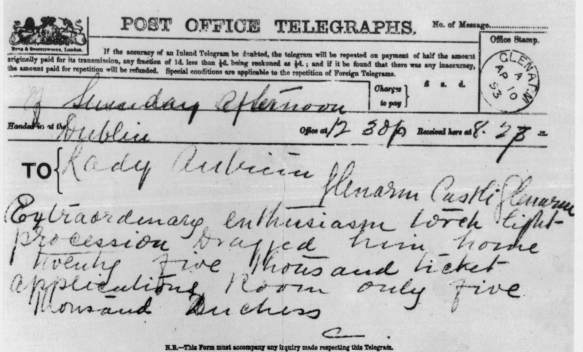

Telegram announcing the overwhelming success of Balfour's Dublin reception.

Lord Salisbury came to Glenarm to lead another Ulster protest. 'Bonfires on the hills looked splendid', wrote Louisa.

The marriage of Princess May and the Duke of York.
At least three of the bridesmaids would have preferred to be the bride.

Alexandra.
Beatrice.
Ena
Drino.
Marie, Countess of Erbach
Princess of Battenberg

Pembroke   Fritz Ponsonby

George Hamilton

Marie Mallet

Conde d'Arnoso 10 N° 1895

A. Pinto Basto 15 Nov 1895

News of the Duke of Argyll's
secret engagement to Ina
McNeill was broken to the
Queen on 30 May 1895.

The dining-room, Balmoral.
Meals were timed for exactly half an hour.

The 'Household' drawing-room at Balmoral, 1895. In November
Louisa overlapped in waiting with Marie Mallet.

The Grandmother of Europe. Queen Victoria photographed with the 'royal mob', as she called them, at Coburg. Princess 'Alicky' and the Tsarevitch are just behind her to the left.

Einladung zur Festtafel

aus Anlaß der Vermählung Ihrer Königlichen Hoheit der Prinzeßin Victoria Melita von Sachsen Coburg Gotha, Herzogin zu Sachsen mit Seiner Königlichen Hoheit dem Großherzoge von Heßen und bei Rhein im Herzoglichen Residenzschloße Ehrenburg am 19 April 1894 um 1 Uhr

für

Palastdame Gräfin Antrim

Der Oberhofmarschall

Queen Victoria kissing her granddaughter after the wedding ceremony. This turned out to be the most disastrous marriage she had ever arranged; the pair divorced in 1901.

Princess Victoria Melita of Edinburgh and the Grand Duke of Hesse. Both were Queen Victoria's grandchildren, and in April 1894 Louisa went with the Queen as Acting Mistress of the Robes to their wedding in Coburg – the Queen's last state visit to Europe.

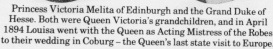

The Queen wore a black corsage covered with diamonds and crossed by the riband of the Garter, a tiara and necklace of diamonds, and a skirt draped with lace and terminating in a long black train. The Emperor wore the uniform of a General of Prussian Infantry in compliment to the bridegroom, who had been raised to the same rank in honour of the occasion; while His Majesty's companion, the Duchess of Coburg, was arrayed in a rich velvet robe of crushed strawberry colour, a tiara of diamonds, and a necklace of pearls. The Prince of Wales had donned the blue tunic of his Royal mother's Dragoon Guards, of which he is also an officer. The bridegroom looked soldierly and handsome in a General of Infantry's uniform, like that of the Emperor; while his blonde and blushing bride was the picture of maidenly beauty in her sumptuous yet simple dress of white satin, trimmed with orange-blossoms. Her two little bridesmaids, one her youngest sister, Princess Beatrice,

The Coburg 'all-male choir' serenading the Queen and the German Emperor and Empress and their suites. The evening had started with the Queen presiding at a family banquet and a torchlight procession outside the Palace.

PROGRAMM.

1. Hochzeitsmarsch a. d. „Sommernachts-
   traum" . . . . *Mendelssohn.*
2. Jubel-Ouverture . . . . *C. M. v. Weber.*
3. Fantasie a. d. Op. „Die Walküre" . . *R. Wagner.*
4. Fackeltanz *von Ihrer Hoheit der Prinzessin Marie von Sachsen-
   Meiningen.*
5. Introduction des 3. Actes und Braut-
   chor a. d. Op. „Lohengrin" . . . . *R. Wagner.*
6. Toréador et Andalouse a. „Bal costumé" *Rubinstein.*
7. Galatea-Walzer *von Sr. Königl. Hoheit dem Herzog Alfred
   von Sachsen Coburg und Gotha.*
8. Fantasie a. d. Op. „Cavalleria rusticana" *Mascagni.*
9. Gavotte: „Blümlein, vergiss mein nicht" *Giese.*
10. Des Grossen Kurfürsten Reiter-
    marsch (Armeemarsch Nr. 213). . *Cuno Graf v. Moltke.*

Music at the state banquet the night before the wedding.

Princess 'Alicky' of Hesse's surprise engagement to the Tsarevitch caused 'general satisfaction', wrote Louisa. Queen Victoria was 'thunderstruck'.

Jendi, le 19. Avril 1894.

Dîner.

Huîtres.
Rossolnik clair.
Petits pâtés à la russe.
Pains de volaille à la Périgueux
Filets de soles frits, Sce. charon.
Selle de mouton à la duchesse.
Vol-au-vent à la financière.
Petits aspics de foie gras.
Pintades rôtis, Salade.
Peches à la Condé.
Glace à la vanille.

Wedding breakfast for the Coburg marriage.

'We watched the newly married pair drive off in a victoria covered with flowers', wrote Louisa.

Sir Henry Ponsonby's daughter, Maggie, and his widow, who was Louisa's aunt.

The death of Sir Henry Ponsonby in November 1895 was a great blow to the Queen. He had succeeded Louisa's father as her Private Secretary in 1870.

The King of Portugal.

BALMORAL.

HER MAJESTY'S DINNER.

Saturday, 9th November, 1895.

POTAGES.
AUX QUENELLES DE GIBIER
AU VOISIN.

POISSONS.
LE TURBOT SAUCE AU VIN.
LES FILETS DE SOLES FRITS.

ENTRÉES.
LA MOUSSE DE VOLAILLE AUX TRUFFES.
LES PERDREAUX À LA STRASBOURGEOISE.

RELEVÉS.
LE BOEUF BRAISE SAUCE PERSIL.
LE JAMBON DE YORK.

RÔTS.
LES DINDES FARCIS. LES POULETS.

ENTREMÊTS.
LES HARICOTS VERTS À LA POULETTE.
LES SAVARINS À LA MONTMORENCY.
LES MERINGUES AU CHOCOLAT.
LES TARTELETTES SUISSES AU FROMAGE.

BUFFET.
COLD FOWL.   COLD BEEF.
TONGUE.

Banquet for the King of Portugal at Balmoral in 1895. 'Fat and pink, just like a prize pig', wrote Marie Mallet, 'and his greediness is quite appalling'.

POST OFFICE TELEGRAPH

Evrae & Spottiswoode, London.

If the accuracy of an Inland Telegram be doubted, the telegram will be repeated on paym... originally paid for its transmission, any fraction of 1d. less than ½d. being reckoned as ½d.; and if it be found that th... the amount paid for repetition will be refunded. Special conditions are applicable to the repetition of Foreign Telegrams.

Charge... to pa...

OHMS

Handed in at the **Osborne** Office at **4:45 ...**

TO { *Countess of Antrim Glenarm ...*

The tell arrived Prince the   *Princess you this succumbed 20th*   *wishes the morning to minnie*   *me dreadful that fever cochrane.*   *news the on*

N.B.—This Form must accompany any inquiry made respecting this Telegram.

DEATH OF
PRINCE HENRY OF BATTENBERG.

Jan 20/96

RECEPTION OF THE NEWS.

SYMPATHY FOR THE QUEEN AND PRINCESS BEATRICE.

THE BODY TO BE BROUGHT HOME.

We deeply regret to announce that Prince Henry of Battenberg died on Monday on board H.M. cruiser Blonde, which was conveying him from Cape Coast Castle to Madeira. The Blonde reached Sierra Leone yesterday morning, and a telegram announcing the Prince's death was received at the Admiralty at about ten o'clock. The sad news was at once telegraphed to the Queen at Osborne, but Her Majesty had already received a telegram direct from Sierra Leone.

Telegram from Princess Beatrice's Lady in Waiting telling Louisa of the death of Prince Henry of Battenberg. He died of fever on the Ashanti expedition.

IN MEMORIAM.

The memorial of the late Prince Henry of Battenberg, of which we are able to give an illustration today, was erected last week by command of the Queen at Craig Dyne, in the Royal Forest of Ballochbuie, near Balmoral. It is a massive monolith—thirteen and a half feet high, four feet wide, and about two and a half feet thick—of red Stirlingshire granite,

Granite monolith erected by the Queen in memory of Prince Henry in the forest near Balmoral.

The Queen at lunch with Princess Beatrice, Prince Henry and their children. 'You, dear Louisa, who have seen our happy life together, can enter into the utter desolation that has come over me', wrote Princess Beatrice.

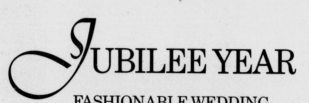

JUBILEE YEAR

FASHIONABLE WEDDING
AT ST. JAMES'S PALACE.
TO THE SOUTH OF FRANCE
WITH THE QUEEN.
CELEBRATIONS AT OSBORNE.
1897

With the new year, excitement returned to Louisa and the Court. Launching her daughter had been Louisa's pleasant occupation between waitings. Now Sybil was to marry. Louisa had chaperoned Sybil at balls, taken her to singing lessons where she shone, and heard that while dining with the Queen 'she did not feel very shy'. Unlike Louisa, she was an intellectual, and according to one of her own daughters, Honor Smith, should have gone to one of the new women's colleges. Instead she became a suffragette. Sir John Balfour was to describe her, in later years, as 'my beautiful and eccentric Godmother'. Meanwhile her 'eccentricity' of the 1890s was to marry into a 'middle-class' and 'rather prosaic' family of bankers, the Smiths. Her son Hugh Vivian Smith was to use this term with pride. But when Lord Antrim took his daughter on his arm up the aisle of St. Margaret's, Westminster, he hissed in her ear, 'You might have married any of Louisa's stuck-up friends, and you go and choose one of these dull, conventional Smiths.' The admonition that Lord Antrim had given to Vivian Smith, on his arrival at Glenarm after becoming engaged to Sybil, was certainly not conventional. 'You can do what you like here, as long as you don't have a woman within seven miles of the Castle.'

The Buzzard avoided spending any unnecessary time in London. Probably for this reason there was no reception after the wedding. But Louisa had a convincing cover-up. Next day, 7 March, she was to accompany Her Majesty to the south of France.

This was Louisa's first taste of foreign travel with Queen Victoria. Her plan of the *Train Spécial* shows that she was to share a compartment with Harriet Phipps, the rattling of whose numerous bangles used to worry the Queen, and whose name was here spelt wrong. A bigger mistake on the part of the management was to imagine that the Household would tolerate the Queen's Indian secretary, the Munshi, in their midst. Despite a scene in which the outraged Queen swept the papers on her writing-table to the floor, the Munshi had to travel separately. When the splendid train, with its buttoned and tasselled upholstery in pale blue, primrose and pearl grey, its elegantly moulded door-handles and ventilators, steamed gently into Nice, unloading took half an hour. There was a mountain of Household baggage, whereas the Indians appeared to carry their all in pocket handkerchiefs. It cost the Queen 80,000 francs (as David Duff in his *Victoria Travels* discovered) for her eight weeks at the Hotel Excelsior Regina, Cimiez. This huge hotel on a hill 'has only been habitable 3 weeks', wrote Louisa, '& smells horribly new'.

The amenities of Cimiez were none the less delightful: basking in a shade temperatue of 68°, listening to music on the Queen's balcony, reading to the Queen in a sheltered corner of the Villa Liserb (lent to her for the sake of privacy) and paying calls on famous personages in other exquisite villas. 'Such a Paradise she has there', wrote Louisa when they lunched at Cap Martin with the Empress Eugénie – still beautiful though dethroned – accompanied by Princess Thora – never beautiful, but a special friend of Louisa's. 'Such a lovely place, Beaulieu, & glorious garden', continued Louisa, after tea with Lady Salisbury. It was Lord Salisbury who made the grand pronouncement on the French Riviera: 'Flies in summer, royalties in winter.' One evening Sir Arthur Bigge took Louisa to Monte Carlo, 'where I proceeded to lose £1'. Bigge must have forgotten that his nickname in the Household was 'Better Not'. Spirits were so high that Louisa was able to record on 1 April, 'Air thick with April Fools'. Indeed Cimiez was altogether 'delicious', except when the air was thick with a *mistral*.

When Louisa came next into waiting the summer of Queen Victoria's Diamond Jubilee was drawing to its sun-drenched close. The royal party, including Princess Thora's sister Marie Louise escaping from her odious husband Prince Aribert, moved to Osborne on 20 July. (Queen Victoria was eventually to rescue Louise from Aribert with a peremptory telegram: 'Tell my granddaughter to come home to me.')

Louisa did not allow the Jubilee celebrations at Osborne to let her forget Princess Beatrice's sorrows. After Liko's death, Princess May had lamented, 'What will the Queen and she do now, those 2 women quite alone . . .?' But royal widows were never 'quite alone'; they had people around them like Louisa. That was one of the things that Ladies in Waiting were for, though all were not as tactful as Louisa. Lady Erroll, for instance, a strict Calvinist, rejoiced when mourning put a stop to theatricals, which she regarded as the devil. She would seize the opportunity to draw her royal mistress's attention to the next world, as when she said to the Queen, 'We will all meet in Abraham's bosom', to which the Queen is said to have retorted, 'I will *not* meet Abraham!' (There is some reason to believe, however, that Louisa's cousin Gerry Liddell, a Lady in Waiting with a keen sense of humour, invented this story, and others like it.) Louisa's approach was more intimate. 'Poor Princess Beatrice's wedding day', she noted on 23 July. 'I went with Minnie to join her at Whippingham [the church where the Battenbergs had married] for an early celebration.'

But the Jubilee must roll forward. There was much dining and lunching in the new Jubilee room at Osborne, designed by Rudyard Kipling's father and known to Louisa as the Indian room, officially as the Durbar room. A loyal address was presented by the people of Newport, followed by another at Cowes, on 27 July. Louisa began this joyful day with her usual writing and reading aloud, perhaps to Princess Beatrice. Later she introduced their luncheon guest, Lady Tennyson. In the old days Lord Tennyson, the Poet Laureate, had had to be coaxed into meeting the Queen, such was his dread of majesty. 'At 10 a.m. to 6 we all went down in carriages & 4 to W. Cowes & waited for the Queen – who came by about 6.30 & had the same function as was at Newport. It looked so pretty, flags etc. & lots of people on the esplanade.'

Cowes was often the scene of international rivalries, when the Emperor William would arrive with an ever bigger and faster yacht, to make sure of beating his Uncle Bertie. But today it was more like a family reunion. Indeed the Jubilee everywhere had been good-tempered. True, a Londoner had shouted 'Hallo, darkie!' at Sir Pertab Singh; but it was a family joke. The crowds at Cowes could almost touch the little old lady, smiling in her carriage. (One of the only two known photographs of Queen Victoria smiling shows her seated in an open carriage, as at Cowes.) 'Sixty Years a Queen!' they exulted. In this old lady were summed up all the hope and glory of a century that was nearing its end.

Back at Glenarm for Christmas, Louisa read a new novel called *The Typewriter Girl*.

EARL AND COUNTESS OF ANTRIM

request the pleasure of

_____

attendance at St. Margaret's Church, Westminster,

on the occasion of their Daughter's marriage,

Saturday, March 6th, at 1.45 p.m.

The first event in Louisa's Jubilee calendar – the engagement of her daughter
Sybil to Vivian Smith, later Lord Bicester. The Buzzard, Louisa's husband, was
'dragged to the slaughter' from Glenarm to the wedding in London.

Glenarm Castle
Co: Antrim
Ireland

Being unfortunately
unable to have a
reception after the
wedding - May I
hope to have the pleasure
of seeing you at
St. James' Palace &c

Invitation to 'view the presents' before the wedding, a standard
Victorian social event. 'Countless hordes of friends' arrived at the
apartment in St. James's Palace lent by Sir Arthur Bigge,
but there was not enough room for a full reception.

**FORTHCOMING FASHIONABLE WED-
DING.**
The marriage of Lady Sybil M. M'Donnell,
daughter of the Earl of Antrim, and niece of Mr.
Schomberg M'Donnell, C.B., private secretary
to Lord Salisbury, and Mr. Vivian Smith, of
Rockhampton and London, will be solemnised at
the Church of St. Margaret, Westminster, S.W.,
on Saturday, 6th March, at 2 p.m. In connection with the event Lord and Lady Antrim entertained all their employes to a sumptuous tea
on Monday last (when the wedding gifts, which
were very numerous and costly, were on view in
the castle), after which dancing, &c, was kept
up till a late hour, all separating with hearty
wishes for long life and happiness to the young
couple.

Angleterre

The
Countess of Antrim
Glenarm Castle
Co Antrim
Ireland

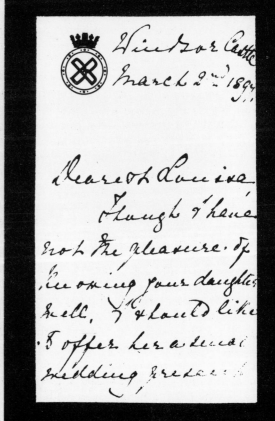

Windsor Castle
March 2nd 1897

Dearest Louisa
Though I have
not the pleasure of
knowing your daughter
well, I should like
to offer her a small
wedding present

Princess Beatrice's letter sending Sybil her present of
an ebony and ormolu clock. The black borders of her letters
were now as wide as the Queen's.

The marriage of Lady Sybil McDonnell to Mr.
Vyvian Smith takes place on Saturday, March 6,
at St. Margaret's, Westminster. The Countess
of Antrim holds a reception at St. James's Palace
the day before to show Lady Sybil's presents.

ST. MARGARET'S CHURCH,

WESTMINSTER.

MARCH 6TH, 1897.

Louisa's and Sybil's costumes for the wedding.

The marriage took place at the most fashionable church in London.

The Archbishop of Armagh, who conducted the service. He was a close friend of the Antrims.

FASHIONABLE MARRIAGE.

MR. VIVIAN H. SMITH—LADY SYBIL MARY McDONNELL.

The marriage took place this afternoon, at the Church of St. Margaret's, Westminster, of Mr. Vivian Hugh Smith, eldest son of Mr. Hugh Colin Smith, one of her Majesty's Lieutenants for the City of London and a director of the Bank of England, of Mount Clare, Roehampton, and Prince's-gate, and Lady Sybil Mary McDonnell, only daughter of the Earl and Countess of Antrim. The Primate of All Ireland, the Archbishop of Armagh (William Alexander, D.D.), officiated, assisted by the Rev. and Hon. Alberic Edward Bertie (rector of Gedling, Notts), uncle of the bride, the Rev. Edgar Sheppard, Sub-Dean of the Chapels Royal, and the Rev. E. Pleydell. The Earl of Antrim gave his daughter away. The bridegroom was supported by his brother, Mr. Launcelot Hugh Smith, as best man. The bride's dress was of plain white moiré velours, with full Court train elegantly trimmed with fine old family Brussels lace. She wore a long Brussels lace veil over orange-blossoms, and she carried a bridal bouquet of rare white exotics. There were no fewer than ten bridesmaids—Miss Olive Hugh Smith (sister of the bridegroom), Miss Marjorie Smith (cousin of the bridegroom); Lady Victoria Sybil Mary Grey (eldest daughter of Earl and Countess Grey), Miss Margaret Dawnay and Miss Marion Vere Dawnay (daughters of the Hon. Lewis and Mrs. Dawnay), Lady Ruby Florence Mary Elliot (second daughter of the Earl and Countess of Minto), Lady Alexandra De Vere Beauclerk (daughter of the Duke and Duchess of St. Albans), and Miss Joan Mabel Howard (daughter of Mr. Henry and Lady Mabel Howard), all cousins of the bride; the Hon. Lilian Theresa Claire Baring (daughter of the Dowager-Lady Ashburton), and the Hon. Elsie Grosvenor (daughter of Lord Stalbridge). There was a very large attendance at the church. Mr. Vivian and Lady Sybil Smith left early in the afternoon for Buxted Park, lent by the Dowager-Lady Ashburton. The presents—between four and five hundred—included, from the Queen (the Countess of Antrim being one of her Ladies-in-Waiting), a jewelled and enamelled pendant, in a design of shamrock, rose, and thistle. The English flower is in pink enamel with a diamond and ruby centre, the Scotch in emerald and diamonds, and the Irish native shamrocks in enamel dew-dropped with diamonds. Princess Henry of Battenberg's present was a unique little ormolu and ebony clock with two carved ivory figures at base.

List of the wedding presents. Victorian readers delighted in these details.

The bridesmaids – mostly from Louisa's vast family.

Pavillon de
S. M. la Reine d'Angleterre

The new Hotel Excelsior where the Queen and her staff stayed. Huge and white, it was described by Lady Lytton as 'an insult to dear old Cimiez'.

The Queen's balcony, photographed by Louisa.

Voyage de Madame la Comtesse DE BALMORAL

Marche-Route
de
CHERBOURG à NICE

STATIONS	HEURES d'arrivée	TEMPS d'arrêt	HEURES de départ	STATIONS	HEURES d'arrivée	TEMPS d'arrêt	HEURES de départ
	h. m.	h. m.	h. m.		h. m.	h. m.	h. m.
Le Jeudi 11 Mars 1897.							
					matin		matin
CHERBOURG ..... Dép.	matin	—	10.25	Mâcon	2.21	3	2.24
Lison	midi 4	5	midi 9	Lyon	3.33	5	3.38
Caen	1.12	6	1.18	Valence	5.19	3	5.22
Lisieux	2.9	4	2.13	Avignon	7.12	55	8.7
Conches	3.19	4	3.23	Tarascon	8.30	1'15	9.45
Mantes	4.34	15	4.49	Marseille (bifurcation de Toulon)	11.23	10	11.33
Noisy-le-Sec	5.58	15	6.13	Toulon	midi 45	5	midi 50
Villeneuve-St-Georges (Triage)	6.46	7	6.53	Les Arcs	2.5	5	2.10
Laroche	9.6	43	9.49	Cannes	3.7	5	3.12
Les Laumes	11.18	8	11.26	NICE .... Arr.	3.45	—	soir
Dijon	nit 21	5	nit 26	Le Vendredi 12 Mars 1897.			

Louisa's first trip to the south of France with Queen Victoria, who travelled 'incognito' as the 'Comtesse de Balmoral'. The journey took 18 hours because of all the stops.

The Queen driving through Nice with her *Chasseurs d'Afrique* behind.

The Queen's special entrance to the Hotel Excelsior Regina.

Queen Victoria in the garden at the Villa Liserb, photographed by Louisa.

Palm trees in Nice. Louisa revelled in the sun.

Three of the Queen's staff; l. to r., Sir Fleetwood Edwards,
Colonel Carington, Fritz Ponsonby.

Louisa walking beside the Queen's pony-cart.

Louisa's pass for the hotel.

The Queen's room. It had red wallpaper and
pictures lent by a dealer in Nice.

Princess Christian on the
Prince of Wales's yacht *Surprise*.

EXCELSIOR HOTEL REGINA

Samedi 3 Avril 1897

A 7 h. 3/4

DANS LA SALLE DES FÊTES

GRANDE

Soirée de Gala

SOUS LE PATRONAGE DE

LA FAMILLE ROYALE D'ANGLETERRE

PREMIÈRE PARTIE

M. SOULACROIX, du Théâtre National de l'Opéra-Comique

Air de la Coupe du Roi de Thulé. DEAZE
A. *Vieille Chanson* . . . . MESSAYEN
B. *La Rosilla* . . . . PRADIER

Mᶨᶫᵉ BERTHELLY, du Théâtre National de l'Opéra-Comique

Variations de Proch

DEUXIÈME PARTIE

Miss ADA THOMPSON, dans ses danses
serpentines

1º *Les Serpents* | 3º *La Papillonne*
2º *Espana* | 4º *La Camé.éonia*

TROISIÈME PARTIE

Mᶨᶫᵉ BERTHELLY & M. SOULACROIX

Duo de la Flûte enchantée . . . . MOZART

Gala evening at the Excelsior.

Rumpelmeyer's in Monte Carlo.
When not needed the staff would
escape there for tea and to gamble
at the casino. Louisa 'lost ten
francs in the beastly place'.

Interior of the Excelsior, which
smelt 'horribly new', wrote Louisa.

The drive to Villefranche.

The Prince of Wales's yacht *Britannia*.

Visit to Lady Salisbury at her villa at Beaulieu.

Expedition to Mentone to open the Jubilee fountain.

Lunch with the Empress Eugénie (right) at Cap Martin. Louisa described her villa as 'a paradise'. The Empress and the Queen were old friends.

La Gruette. Louisa went on a tour of the Loire châteaux on her way home.

The fountain at Mentone which was officially opened by Princess Victoria in honour of the Queen's Jubilee.

Water Supplies TO Country Mansions.

1898

"THE CHATEAU MALET," MONTE CARLO.
Water Supply, Fire Protection, and Electric Light by
Merryweather

Above: Azay-le-Rideau on the Loire.
Left: an up-to-date 'château' at Monte Carlo.

The Queen starting for the Jubilee celebrations at Cowes.

Fritz Ponsonby, the Queen's equerry.

1837   1897

THE

DIAMOND ✳ JUBILEE.

Visit to Cowes

OF

HER MOST GRACIOUS MAJESTY

THE QUEEN,

AND

Presentation of Address.

TUESDAY, JULY 27th, 1897.

PROGRAMME

PRINTED BY GEO. FELLOWS, "HERALD" OFFICE, COWES.

The Queen arriving at Cowes.

Programme for the Jubilee celebrations at Cowes. Louisa went
down to Osborne with the Queen the week before.

Driving through Cowes. 'Lots of flags and
lots of people', wrote Louisa.

Yachts in the harbour at Cowes. Louisa enjoyed
'fizzing' from Osborne to here by boat.

The Durbar Room at Osborne. Built for the Jubilee, it had Indian hangings and was lit by bulbs in large blue Indian vases.

Louisa with her camera, surrounded by members of the Royal Household.

The Queen going to breakfast at Osborne. She liked to eat out in the garden under a green-fringed parasol tent.

A Jubilee recital for the Queen: Plançon and Ben Davies, sketched by Aline Majendie.

Princess Thora, daughter of Princess Christian, with two of Princess Beatrice's children at Osborne, 1897. She became a great friend of Louisa.

HOUSEPARTIES AND HEROES

BALMORAL AND WINDSOR.
LAST VISIT TO THE
VILLA LISERB.
1898-1899

These two years were to be Louisa's last with the Queen at Cimiez. The journey of 1898 produced an innovation: the royal party travelled down to Portsmouth in the 'new corridor train', Louisa and Harriet, who shared a compartment, no doubt rejoicing that there were no more of those embarrassing stops at wayside stations for a visit to the 'Ladies'. Queen Victoria could have ordered corridor trains much earlier, had she not dreaded their increased speed. The crossing to Cherbourg on the royal yacht *Victoria & Albert* was atrocious, the weather-men having misled H.M. about the wind. Louisa, not sea-sick herself, remarked that the crossing 'upset a good many people'. One of the many was Queen Victoria, who described herself as 'feeling much upset' after the port-hole burst open and the sea, together with a horrified crowd of maids, stewards and footmen, 'all rushed in'.

Louisa as usual found Nice 'so bright and & pretty & *warm*. Streets crowded all the way & an escort etc. reception most enthusiastic' – this in spite of the fact that Anglo-French relations were approaching their nadir. The Fashoda incident was about to explode. Meanwhile, Queen Victoria had not helped matters by ordering Bertie to receive President Faure of the French Republic on the stairs instead of at the door of the hotel. A President did not merit a Sovereign's welcome. Nice was 'crawling with royalties', complained Marie Mallet. Among them was the Grand Duchess of Mecklenburg-Strelitz; the sad tale of her daughter's seduction by a footman was poured out to the Queen, 'so we had to hang about', wrote Louisa. Perhaps to make up for this, the Queen gave her 'a dear little locket'. (Most of Harriet's irritating bangles were similar gifts.) And there was always Rumpelmeyer's, where the Household would lap up cream floating on delicious chocolate.

The hero of Cimiez 1899 was Sir James Reid, the Queen's physician. He shared with Princess May the honour of receiving a smacking kiss from the queen of the Nice flower-sellers. Later the same year he was to make history by wringing a smile from Majesty over a Household marriage. Fritz Ponsonby had failed signally over his own marriage; the Queen even refused to let him begin his married life in the Saxon Tower. What would happen when 'Jamie' Reid announced his engagement to a Maid of Honour, Louisa's cousin Susan Baring? Reid promised 'never to do it again' – and Her Majesty had to smile. Maurice Baring had earlier arranged entertainments for the royal party in Paris, where they stayed at the Hotel Wagram. He took his cousin Louisa and Princess Christian to a 'café luncheon' – another innovation that Lord Ribblesdale considered responsible for the cheerfulness of the Naughty Nineties. Louisa often criticized the theatre. She had pronounced *The Little Minister* by J.M.Barrie '*quite* the worst play I have ever seen'. But Baring's choice of the *risqué* French comedy, *Les Femmes chez Maxime*, was, even in Louisa's discreet diary, 'awful'.

Lord Kitchener, the Sirdar of Egypt, had been the hero of Balmoral in 1898. He was invited to stay there after his double triumph in the Sudan: at Omdurman against the Dervishes in September – 'a splendid performance', wrote Louisa, as if describing an athletic contest between equals; and at Fashoda in November when Kitchener's show of strength forced the French to withdraw. Louisa sat next to the Sirdar at dinner, but characteristically refrained from recording a word he said. Marie Mallet was in raptures over his ability to 'talk intelligently on all subjects'. And little Alick Yorke was on tiptoe to amuse the hero when a Maid of Honour sketched them out walking.

Another hero at Balmoral was still Mr Balfour, 'Old Gladstone' having been sent to Valhalla without achieving Home Rule. Balfour had once been convicted of 'telling a fib' to H.M. when he denied having played golf on the Sabbath. Now the Queen teased him as he shouldered his clubs with a soulful expression. One visitor that winter seemed no heroine in the Household's eyes. Princess Lobanov defended the current pogroms in Russia on the ground that Jews were merely 'little heaps of dust and rags'. The sentence of Colonel Dreyfus had shocked everybody. 'Dreyfus was condemned to 10 yrs. imprisonment to France's eternal disgrace', Louisa wrote on 9 September; and later, 'The papers thrilling & speaking of the intense indignation roused universally by Dreyfus verdict'. While bringing Sybil's family records up to date, Louisa stuck in a telegram about Dreyfus. Sybil's daughter Honor Smith, however, believes that Louisa's political enthusiasms, whether for Dreyfus or against Home Rule, were matters of empathy rather than principle. She simply absorbed and reproduced the atmosphere at Court.

Sybil was by now the mother of two. Her son Rufus, a pretty child, had won the Buzzard's rare approval, as Louisa was happy to record: 'Bill now takes tremendous notice of Rufus.' During these years the ties of family and friends pulled at Louisa's heart, in competition with her duty to the Queen. Her own health was never weighed against the Queen's comfort. On the very last visit to Cimiez, Louisa and another of the Queen's ladies, Victoria Grant, went down with feverish chills. Or, rather, they refused to 'go down' until the eleventh hour. By 8 April Louisa was 'so C.D.' [seedy] that she had to 'beg off dinner'. Two days later she was at dinner again, but 'rather terrified' of having to picnic with the Queen. It was the same with Victoria Grant. 'Poor Victoria was bad again in the afternoon & evening & it ended in the Queen having to know about it.' What with 'futile shopping' and days of 'shaking' after sleepless nights, Louisa was relieved to write: 'Windsor . . . 6 weeks since I left England & very glad to get home.'

Home always meant a good deal of time at Glenarm ('Bill glad to see me', she would notice), but also delightful family gatherings in both England and Scotland, and grand houseparties. She adored her sisters, continually referring to the pleasure of being 'all together again'. At a Clandeboye houseparty, the brilliant Lord Dufferin, lately Viceroy of India, took her walking round his romantic lake, and to see the 'glorious view' from Helen's Tower. At Panshanger she went walking with Lord Cowper, but did not mention in her diary his wonderful collection of pictures. Probably the most amusing houseparty was at Beningbrough, where 'Mr Sykes gave some excellent imitations'. This was the Christopher Sykes who was the obsequious butt of the Prince of Wales and who received splashes of brandy down his neck, while crawling round under the table, with the formula, 'As your Royal Highness pleases'.

Louisa herself was an excellent mimic. A favourite story told to her grandchildren was of Queen Victoria, a royal grandchild and Louisa driving at Windsor. 'Gangan, may we see the copper horse?' '*Not* the "copper horse",' corrected the Queen; 'the statue of your great-great-grandfather King George III.'

Balmoral in the snow, Autumn 1898. Lord Kitchener, the nation's hero, and some of Louisa's greatest friends at Court were staying, so she much enjoyed this 'waiting'.

THE FIGHT
FOR
KHARTOUM.

———

GREAT BRITISH VICTORY.

———

15,000 DERVISHES SLAIN.

———

BRITISH LOSS 300.

———

KHALIFA'S FLIGHT.

———

Kitchener

Lord Kitchener, the Sirdar, fresh from his triumph at Fashoda. The Queen was so taken with him that she invited him to sit down in her presence

BALMORAL, THURSDAY.

The Queen went out yesterday morning with Princess Henry of Battenberg.

In the afternoon her Majesty drove, attended by the Countess of Antrim and the Hon. Mrs. Mallet.

Her Royal Highness the Duchess of Fife and the Duke of Fife arrived at the Castle from Mar Lodge.

Mr. Balfour had the honour of dining with the Queen.

In the evening Madame Blanche Marchesi (Baroness Caccamisi) and M. Hollman had the honour of performing the following selection of music before her Majesty and the Royal Family :

Violoncello Fantaisie, " Carmen "		Arr. by Hollman.
M. Hollman.		
Songs { " Die Lorelei "		Liszt.
" Wiegenlied "		Mozart.
Madame Marchesi.		
Violoncello { Aria		Schumann.
Mazurka		Chopin.
Papillon		Popper.
M. Hollman.		
Songs { " Nussbaum "		Schumann.
" O Cessate di piagarmi "		Scarlatti.
" L'amour est un enfant trompeur "		Martini.
Madame Marchesi.		
Violoncello { " Le Cygne "		Saint-Saëns.
Serenade		Hollman.
M. Hollman.		
Songs { " Myrte "		Délibes.
" Tu me disais "		Chaminade.
" Chant Vénitien "		Bemberg.
Madame Marchesi.		

The concert starring Madame Marchesi. Louisa described it as 'most lovely', but Madame Marchesi's husband, Baron Caccamisi, proved himself to be a 'fierce Sicilian'.

un ill assorted couple

Aline Majendie
Nov. 1st 1898

Lord Kitchener and Alick Yorke sketched by Aline Majendie. Alick Yorke, Groom in Waiting, was unofficial Court jester.

Aline Majendie, Maid of Honour, 'Court cartoonist' and a close friend of Louisa.

Smoking at Balmoral. In earlier times Queen Victoria would have forbidden it.

10.30 p.m. Balmoral Drawingroom -

Aline Majendie
June 14
1899

The ordeal of the Queen's drawing-room after dinner,
drawn by Aline Majendie.

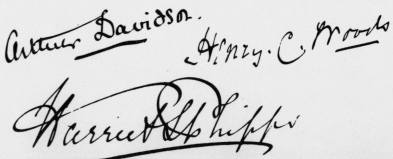

Arthur Davidson.   Henry C. Woods

Harriet Phipps

Above: Harriet Phipps
and Victoria Grant.
Left: Princess Clementine
amusing the Household.

Jokes on the terrace – photos by Louisa.

Aline Majendie

J H Liddell;
15th June 1899

"Ne vous derangez pas"

I began to feel uneasy.
When the Baron Caccamisi
Both furious & greasy,
Knocked at my chamber door,
& my heart began to beat.
For with nothing on my feet
& wrapped in a bath sheet
I stood upon the floor

But I flung the portal wide
& standing by my side
With no attempt to hide
was the wild Sicilian bore

"C'est moi Monsieur. Ha! Ha!
Vous voyez je suis là
Le Baron de Cacca
Ne vous derangez pas
Vous pourrez à peine croire
Que je suis au désespoir
Car je veux ma femme revoir
Mais ne vous derangez pas"

Oh do not thus repine.
But won't you stop and dine?
Os take a glass of wine?
"Ne vous derangez pas"

Your wife is well & bright
Her singing is quite! quite!
We hoped she'd stay the night
Ne vous derangez pas.

Non Monsieur je ne veux.
C'est impossible que je peux.
Nous sommes toujours à deux
Ne vous derangez pas.

Souvenir of Madame Marchesi's
Visit to Balmoral. Nov. 1898.

Aleck   Balmoral

Alick Yorke's poem describing his narrow escape from Madame Marchesi's husband, who was prowling the corridors in search of his wife.

Balmoral, Summer 1899.
Louisa's last but one visit.

Princess Thora. Like Louisa, she was a keen cyclist.

Princesses Thora and
Clementine of Belgium.

The Queen at seventy-nine, and
in 'excellent spirits'.

3 Oh Royal heart, with wide embrace
  For all her children yearning !
Oh happy realm, such mother-grace
  With loyal love returning !
Where England's flag flies wide unfurl'd,
  All tyrant wrongs repelling ;
God make the world a better world
  For man's brief earthly dwelling !

The Queen's Diamond Jubilee
hymn, composed by Arthur
Sullivan. It was sung to her
every year on her anniversary.

Sir James Reid, the Queen's
doctor. She was much annoyed
in 1899 when he became
engaged to Susan Baring,
a Maid of Honour
and Louisa's cousin.

"10 MINUTES TO
WAT, TONS OF
TIME FOR A
GAME

A.J. Balfour, the deputy Prime Minister. The Queen
laughed at his addiction to golf.

[Copyright.]

HYMN

RITTEN BY

THE BISHOP OF WAKEFIELD,

AND SET TO MUSIC BY

ARTHUR SULLIVAN,

(By Request)

TO BE USED

In all Churches and Chapels in England and Wales,
and in the Town of Berwick-upon-Tweed,

UPON

Sunday the Twentieth Day of June 1897,

*As forming part of the Service authorised to
be used on that day.*

LONDON:
Printed by EYRE and SPOTTISWOODE,
Printers to the Queen's most Excellent Majesty.
1897.

Windsor, 1898. The houseparty included the Empress Frederick, Lord Salisbury and the Grand Duke Serge, uncle of the Tsar (he was assassinated in 1905).

Princess Beatrice.

Lord Salisbury.

Princess Lobanov Rosteovsky and Elizabeth, the Grand Duchess.

Dreyfus's prison on Devil's Island.

Alfred Dreyfus, the *cause célèbre* of 1898.

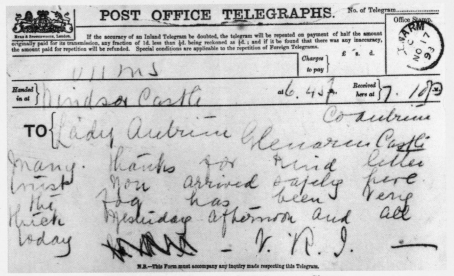
Telegram from the Queen after Louisa's return to Glenarm.

(beloved) *March*

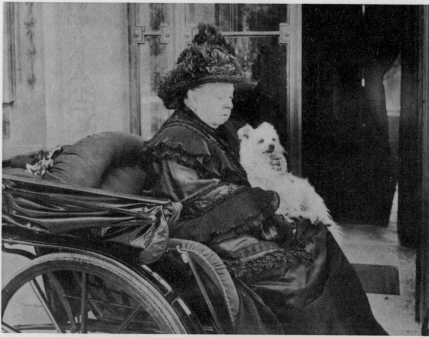

Princess Helena. She sensibly
did not mention the play to
Queen Victoria.

Queen Victoria in the garden at the Villa Liserb. She gave Louisa
this photograph as a remembrance.

A trip to Paris with Princess Helena, Spring 1899.
Maurice Baring took them both to a *risqué* French play.
'Too appalling for words', confided Louisa to Marie Mallet.

Louisa's last visit to the south of France with the Queen.
The Hotel Excelsior was 'literally crawling with royalties',
wrote Marie Mallet.

Leoncavallo, sketched by Fritz
Ponsonby when he sang to the
Queen, 27 March 1899.

Hélène de France.
Duchesse d'Aoste.
Avril 1899.

Princess Hélène, Duchess of Aosta. The beautiful daughter of the
Comte de Paris, she had once captured the heart of Prince Eddy,
eldest son of the Prince of Wales.

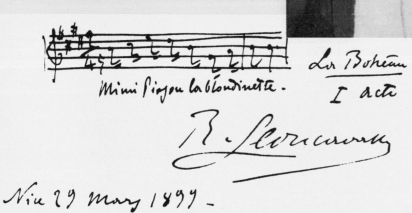

Mimi Pinson la blondinette.
La Bohème
I acte
R. Leoncavallo

Nice 29 May 1899 –

Bar of music written for Louisa by the great Leoncavallo (composer of *I Pagliacci*).

Clara Eissler

Marianne Eissler

Princess Beatrice, the Queen's constant companion in her last years.

Princess May, the Duchess of York, stayed at Cimiez too this year. She went for long drives with the Queen and found her 'most dear and kind'.

The Eissler sisters at a tea-time concert for the Queen.

The concert hall at the Hotel Excelsior.

Octeto Español — 22 Abril 1899
1. Marcha . . . . La Cariñosa . . Cotó
2. Gavota . . . . María Luisita . Echeverría
3. Vals . . . . . Reverie . . . Cotó
4. Fantasía . . . Jolie Fille de Perth . Bizet
5. Danzas Españolas { a Seguidillas Manchegas
                     { b Panadera (Sevilla) . Oró
6. Tango . . . . El Abanico . . Cotó
7. Polca Mazurca . La Filumena . Alberto
8. Gran Vals Español . . . . Alberto

Marcha Real Española

Dios Salve la Reina

Rousing Spanish music for the Queen from the Eissler sisters.

Picnic stop by the roadside above Cimiez – a relief for the Queen's Scottish gillie, who had to pant up hills after the royal carriage.

From Villa Cyrnos
M. Ilchester - Cap Martin

View of Cap Martin from the Empress Eugénie's villa.

BOERS AND IRISH

BALMORAL
DUBLIN AND GLENARM.
1899-1900

Those two small peoples, the Boers and the Irish, would have seemed equally troublesome – until 1899. Queen Victoria called the Boers 'most merciless and cruel', while the Buzzard knew all about the Irish Fenians. During a period of Fenian violence, he arrived one day direct from Ireland for a Parliamentary committee. The policeman on duty outside the Houses of Parliament asked what was inside his Gladstone bag. 'Dynamite!' yelled the Buzzard, 'All lie down!' and he hurled the bag high into the air and himself flat on the ground. But by the end of 1899 the perspective had changed at least in the Queen's mind. The Boers seemed to her worse than ever; no less cruel to the natives, but now a threat to her territories in South Africa. Whereas the loyal Irish regiments were fighting like the devil in H.M.'s forces. This reversal would mean a radical change in the Queen's spring schedule.

The Boer War broke out in October 1899. At first Louisa was her usual optimistic self. 'Balmoral. 20 October. Magnificent fight in the Transvaal . . . a brilliant victory.' Not so Queen Victoria. Three days later Louisa was writing, 'The Queen so nice but much occupied by rather anxious news from Natal'. By the end of November Louisa was only hoping that familiar names and special people would survive. 'I was in an awful state of mind all day getting no news of casualties but at last mercifully telegram came with no familiar name on the list – one could breathe again.' Prince Christian Victor ('Christle') of Schleswig-Holstein was among the special people. Both his mother Princess Christian and his sister Thora had sent Louisa agonized messages. '*You* know what that precious boy means to me,' wrote his mother. 'Is not this a time of terrible anxiety?' wrote Thora, ' . . . my very special brother is now soon arriving at the Cape.'

Then they were into Black Week, and the Queen was stiffening a gloomy Mr Balfour. 'Please understand that there is no one depressed in this house . . .' But Louisa, who was no longer in that vigorous house but in jittery London, frankly admitted her depression. '13 December. We heard Ist. rumour of Ld.Methuen's repulse at Modders Fontein. This naturally threw us into the depths.' She was at Glenarm for the New Year, hanging like everyone else on the news of beleaguered British armies in South Africa. '10 January. No fresh war news & the state of public tension great.' '26 January. A terrible blow getting a telegram to say Spion Kop was abandoned after our very hard day's fighting. So we are where we were before – & depression all the greater . . . I went out in the afternoon & dug at the nettles'. (As if they were Boers, perhaps.) And at Osborne, the knitting-needles with which the Queen used to conduct duets after dinner in the Excelsior were now knitting comforters for the troops.

Queen Victoria had taken her grand decision. It was to visit Ireland; that prodigal son she had not seen for almost forty years, but who now deserved the fatted calf. Her motivation in choosing Ireland rather than France for her spring holiday was well understood. She could hardly go to Cimiez with the French press spitting about the war. She might even be assassinated. The Empress of Austria had already been killed by a terrorist and the King of Italy was soon also to meet this fate. But her own police could be relied upon to protect her in Ireland and keep ugly Fenian noises off-stage. To a daughter, she wrote: 'It was entirely my own idea as was also my giving up going

abroad – and it will give great pleasure and do good.' To a Lady in Waiting she added in a burst of candour: 'I must honestly confess it is *not* entirely to please the Irish but because I expect to enjoy myself.'

She did not enjoy the crossing. Everyone was sea-sick from Queen to chef, except Louisa. She described the voyage with the maddening complacency of a good sailor: 'Comfortable journey though blowy – ladies' dinner on board.' Perhaps she should have written 'overboard'. These horrors were the prelude to a magnificent triumph. 'Mercifully a fine day', Louisa wrote on their arrival, '& splendid for the Queen's reception.' They did not reach Viceregal Lodge till two, 'quite stupid & dazed with exhaustion; but everything had been most successful'.

Most of the royal progresses were 'really wonderful', despite the horses' sometimes 'pulling so dreadfully' when frightened by the banshee screams of joy. Louisa only once allowed herself to mention the dark side: on 6 April, 'a hideous drive through squalid streets'. Fritz Ponsonby noticed that these streets were not decorated, or their decorations were vandalized. But when the Queen was greeted in Phoenix Park by fifty-two thousand children from all over Ireland, Louisa pronounced the clamour 'positively deafening'. Great was Her Majesty's satisfaction. She never learnt to distinguish, as Fritz certainly and Louisa probably did, between universal applause, as in Phoenix Park, and cheering tempered by the 'droning bagpipe' of boos at the back of other crowds.

One alarmist idea was effectively dispelled. An officer's wife in Dublin named Clara Armstrong had fervently hoped Louisa would use her influence with H.M. to make her sport the outward and visible signs of royalty while inspecting the schoolchildren; otherwise she might not be recognized. 'The Queen's well-known kindness to the little ones may perhaps induce her to wear a jewelled coronet in front of her bonnet, and use at least an ermine carriage rug, to enhance their pleasure' – and establish her own identity. But in no time the Queen's small, round, black figure was known all over Ireland. There was no need to wear 'an ermine-lined robe thrown back in folds', as Mrs Armstrong further suggested. Far less a crown precariously 'surmounting her bonnet', for ever since her Golden Jubilee the bonnet had been the symbol of her maternal rule. The Princess of Wales had failed to make her wear a crown out of doors in 1887; Mrs Armstrong was not likely to succeed now.

Louisa went home halfway through the Irish visit to be with her family at Easter. She was at Glenarm during much of the last Victorian summer. Her silver wedding day was on 1 June: 'Lots of letters & telegrams & a promise of presents.' But Buzzard's refusal to appear during the Queen's Irish visit had made Louisa fearful lest all the McDonnells should be *persona non grata* at Court. So when in June the Queen asked her to use her influence with Pom McDonnell (now on active service in South Africa), to get him back as Lord Salisbury's Private Secretary, Louisa hastened to obey. She wrote to Pom: 'I am so afraid Buzz not coming to Dublin will make her think the family cranky.' And how could anyone resist, after H.M. had written to Louisa, as she did, 'Lord Salisbury's present secretary is *not* the man required'? Pom dutifully arranged to return in October. Meanwhile the successful Louisa, photographed between two stone pillars on the steps at Glenarm, was every inch Queen of her own castle.

SUCH A SURPRISE.

MR. BALFOUR: "Fancy, Ridley! they've actually got horses!"
SIR M. W. RIDLEY: "And look, Arthur, they've got rifles, too! What a shame to deceive us!"

Cartoon by Carruthers Gould – a skit on the Government's surprise
at finding the Boers so well equipped to fight.

The Queen at Balmoral,
22 October 1899, sending her
sympathy for 'the dreadful
losses' at the Battle of Glencoe.
The Boer War had begun
ten days before.

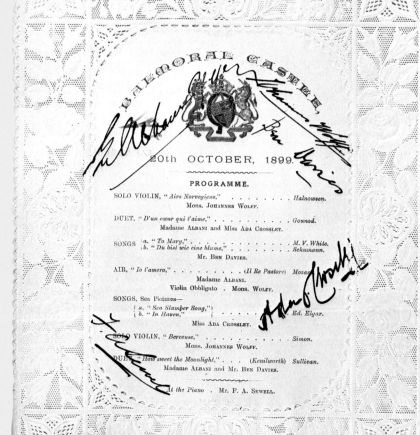

'Pom' McDonnell, Louisa's brother-in-law and
Lord Salisbury's Private Secretary since 1888. He enlisted in the
City Imperial Volunteers, and the Queen sent an urgent message
through Louisa, begging him to return.

Lt. McDonnell 'Boerwatching' with a fellow officer at the front.

Madame Albani's concert at
Balmoral. It failed to lighten
the general gloom.

Hearty Christmas Greetings

and Best Wishes

from

1899

Edward

Albert

Victoria Mary

Louisa's last Christmas card from the Queen, 1899.

Princess May with her children.

The three eldest York children, Prince Edward, Princess Mary and Prince Albert.

THE ABSENT-MINDED BEGGAR

· BY ·

RUDYARD KIPLING.

Kipling's famous poem written to raise money for the troops in the Boer War.

Cecil Rhodes besieged in Kimberley.

Colonel Kekewitch, the commanding officer in Kimberley.

The martial spirit. Louisa's nephews and nieces dressed up as soldiers, Christmas 1899.

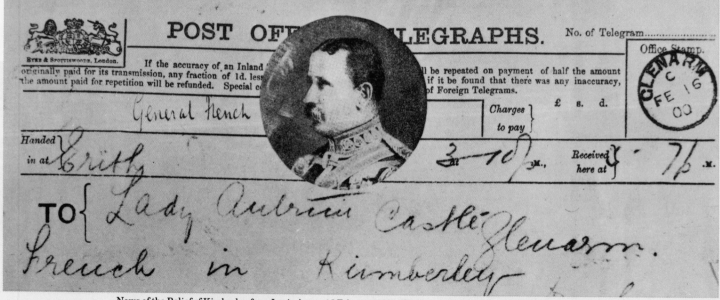

News of the Relief of Kimberley from Louisa's son, 16 February 1900. 'Such a comfort', she wrote in her diary at Glenarm.

POST OFFICE TELEGRAPHS.

If the accuracy of an Inland Telegram be doubted, the telegram will be repeated on payment of half the amount ... nsmission, any fraction of 1d. less than ½d. being reckoned as ½d.; and if it be found that there was any inaccuracy ... etition will be refunded. Special conditions are applicable to the repetition of Foreign Telegrams.

No. of Telegram..........

Feb. 28 1900

Handed in at Gloster Rd

£ s. d.

Charges to pay

at 9-25ª .M., Received here at 10·12

TO { Austria

Glenarm Ireland
Ladysmith- relieved cavalry entered
last- night Sybil

The Relief of Ladysmith.
A telegram from Louisa's
daughter Sybil.

O Terence, dear, and did you hear
The news that's going round?
The shamrock's Erin's badge by law
Where e'er her sons are found.
From Bloemfontein to Ballybank
'Tis ordered by the Queen;
We've won our right in open fight,
The wearin' o' the green.

'The Wearing of the Green',
March 1900. The Queen was so
impressed by Irish gallantry at
the front that she decreed the
wearing of a shamrock on
St.Patrick's day by all Irish
soldiers.

BRAVO! BULLER!
"It's dogged as does it."

Buller's 'triumph'. It took him four months to relieve Ladysmith.

The Queen driving out to review the Guards at Buckingham Palace in March.

Buller's fall. He was replaced as commander by Lord Roberts.

The Horse Guards drawn up in Buckingham Palace Gardens. This was the Queen's last public review.

The Queen's Journey to Ireland April 2 & 3 1900

LONDON AND NORTH WESTERN RAILWAY.

ARRANGEMENT OF CARRIAGES

COMPOSING

HER MAJESTY'S TRAIN

From WINDSOR to HOLYHEAD,

On MONDAY, the 2nd, and TUESDAY, the 3rd APRIL, 1900.

Engine.	Guard.	For Men Servants.	Dressers and Ladies' Maids.	The Countess of Antrim, Hon. Harriet Phipps.	Princess Christian of Schleswig-Holstein.	Queen's Dressers.	Her Majesty and Princess Henry of Battenberg.	Personal Servants.	Sir Fleetwood Edwards, Sir Arthur Bigge, Lt.-Col. Hon. W. Carington, Capt. Ponsonby, Sir James Reid.	Indian Attendants.	For Pages and Upper Servants.	Directors.	Directors.	Guard.
Engine.	Van. No. 210.	Carriage No. 870.	Saloon. No. 73.	Saloon. No. 50.	Saloon. No. 131.		Royal Saloon.		Saloon. No. 153.	Saloon. No. 71.	Saloon. No. 72.	Saloon. No. 180.	Carriage No. 306.	Van. No. 272.

< 341 feet 3 inches > < 271 feet 4 inches >

The Royal Yacht *Victoria & Albert.* 'We got over comfortably', wrote Louisa – but everyone else was seasick.

The Queen's 'special' to Holyhead and Ireland. It was her first visit since 1848, and she told her ladies 'I expect to enjoy myself'.

Procession through Dublin. Louisa arrived at the Viceregal Lodge 'quite stupid and dazed' from the cheers.

Earl Cadogan, the Irish Lord Lieutenant, and his wife.

The Viceregal Lodge in Phoenix Park.

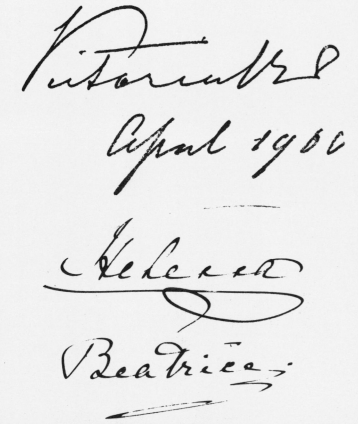

The Queen in her pony-chair. She was drawn round the gardens by a white donkey.

The Duchess of Connaught.

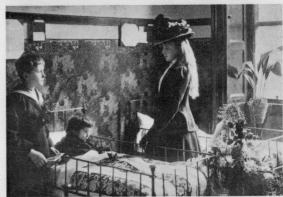

Princess Beatrice's children. Princess Ena and Prince Leopold visited the Children's Hospital in Dublin with Louisa.

The Duke of Connaught,
Commander-in-Chief in Dublin.

The Queen meeting Irish schoolchildren in Phoenix Park.
'The noise was positively deafening', wrote Louisa.

Summer at Glenarm. Louisa returned thankfully to her castle after the hectic 'waitings' in Dublin and London.

Emily G Loch

Ferdy Bentinck

Patrick Bowe & Lyon

Josslyn. S. Egerton.

Jock B. Lyon

Angus McDonnell

Dunluce

Lady Gladys Hamilton.

Lady Gladys Hamilton and Katharine Trefusis in Louisa's garden, August 1900.

The young men setting off to shoot.

Angus McDonnell, Louisa's younger son, on an 'Otto Dicycle'.

Gladys Hamilton

Katharine Trefusis

G.M. Liddell

Katharine Trefusis and the Glenarm cricket eleven on the front steps.

Gerry Liddell, Louisa's cousin.

Gerry Liddell pruning a creeper at Glenarm.

The Barbican tower and bridge over the Glenarm river.

Katharine Trefusis

Sybil with Rufus.

The cricketers after the match. Angus is wearing a straw hat, fourth from left.

Louisa's water-colour of the herbaceous border and greenhouse.

Distant glimpse of towers from the meadow.

The Rose Wilderness at Glenarm.

Garron Tower six miles away from Glenarm.

Rocketing flower borders
in August.

Vere and Rufus, Louisa's grandchildren.

View up the glen, painted by Louisa from her window.

Vere among the hydrangeas.

Rufus on the lawn.

The Buzzard with his grandson.

Nora and Delia Lyttelton in picture hats.

Flower borders in September.

Glenarm village, sketched by Louisa.

Louisa on the steps at Glenarm.

FAREWELL TO THE QUEEN

LAST WAITING
AT WINDSOR.
VOYAGE TO OTTAWA.
THE QUEEN'S FUNERAL.
1900-1901

ouisa's last waiting of 1900 took place during the week 4 to 11 December. She had not seen the Queen since June, when she returned with the Court to Windsor after her fortnight at Balmoral. 'I had breakfast at the Castle', noted Louisa, 'then waited to say goodbye to the Queen.'

When she saw the Queen again there was indeed a melancholy change. She could hardly swallow her arrowroot and milk. 'I have not been feeling very well lately.' Gone were the days when Sir James Reid had tried to cut down her diet. In the south of France he had once entertained her ladies with the remark: 'People who reach eighty go on till they die of old age.' So at eighty-one she was dying. But it was not just old age. The Boer War was a depressant; so was the 'dark gloomy weather', which Louisa charted. The 'poor old swimming bath', wrote the Queen, was wrecked in a summer storm. Louisa had often 'revelled' there. Worst of all, there were two tragic deaths in the royal family: the Queen's son Prince Alfred ('Affie') from cancer, and the idolized Christle from enteric fever. 'He is gone', announced poor Princess Thora in a shaking voice to the Queen; and then tried to comfort her by saying she *knew* 'he was happy'. No one else was. His mother and sister both sent emotional letters to Louisa, Princess Christian's concluding, 'These horrid wicked treacherous Boers – no punishment *can* be too great for that . . . wicked old Kruger'.

The Queen's last romanticized portrait, by Benjamin Constant, was utterly remote from the sad reality. Nevertheless she loved it for its ethereal beauty, and gave a copy to Louisa. She had also shown a touch of her old spirit in sending Constant a piece of Garter ribbon, since he had not got the colour quite right. On opening the parcel, the poor man at first thought she was presenting him with the Most Noble Order itself. Gallantly the Queen tried to keep to her usual routine. She had 'a good day' on 6 December, rejoiced Louisa, and next day the Lyttelton children 'came down in the afternoon to see the Queen drive past'. What a strain those once 'talkative' drives had become. Louisa, like Marie Mallet, might well find the royal head resting on her shoulder, for Majesty often dozed. The erstwhile nuisance of constantly changing her cloaks – 'my thin, my half-thin, my thick', as the Queen used to call them – had now become a valuable ploy for keeping her awake. But one must operate skilfully, so as not to disturb the royal bonnet. On 10 December Louisa said goodbye again, never dreaming that her 'long walk' with Queen Victoria was over. She herself was off to Canada to stay with the Mintos. Just before she sailed on S.S. *Cymric*, the Queen's beloved Lady in Waiting, Jane Churchill, died. 'Thank God Grandmama is no worse for this fresh blow', wrote Thora to Louisa. In fact it was to prove the last straw.

Meanwhile Louisa was 'revelling' once more – in the sparkle of Her Majesty's Viceregal Court at Government House, Ottawa. Her diary overflows with the old zest. She adored the fancy-dress balls, pantomimes and houseparties. Young Winston Churchill was there with Ian Malcolm, Lillie Langtry's future son-in-law: they had just formed the Malcolmtents' Club, but Louisa was never a malcontent. The games of ice-hockey were 'thrilling & exciting'; even the moonlight seemed more brilliant than usual, in the intense cold. And it was heart-warming to receive Her Majesty's telegram (sent by Harriet Phipps) on 8 January: 'Osborne. Queen hopes you are well glad arrived

safe was passage bad.' That particular passage could always be bad, as a sketch by Louisa's son, Ducie, shows (see page 108).

Alas, the next telegram from England was less cheerful. '19 January. A bad account of the Queen gave me the most awful ridge – I am afraid she is very ill.' Next day's reports were 'most alarming' and on 22 January Louisa wrote: 'So saddened by news that the Queen was sinking . . . Such an *iron* ridge – it is such a break up.' Queen Victoria died at Osborne that evening, 'surrounded by her children and grandchildren', according to the official bulletin. One of those children was Louisa's friend Princess Christian. In thanking Louisa for her heartfelt sympathy, the Princess wrote down on 2 February her own impression (hitherto unpublished) of her mother's last moments: 'I shall never forget the look of radiance on her face at last when she opened her dear eyes quite wide – & one *felt* & knew she saw beyond the Border Land – & had *seen* & *met* all *her loved ones*. In death she was so beautiful, such peace & joy on her dear face – a radiance from Heaven.' The Queen's chaplain, Randall Davidson, had himself observed the 'change' but did not describe it.

Princess Thora was also to thank Louisa on 2 February in telling words: 'I know you of all others would be able to realize what the loss of darling Grandmama is to me.' Louisa's own granddaughter was later to pinpoint Louisa's extraordinary gift of sympathy as the secret of her success. Though not especially witty or clever, she possessed charm and warmth that enabled her to get on with everybody: 'She made these wonderful sort of cooing, purring noises, "Mmm, do go on – I do understand, mmm." She could always be trusted to thaw out difficult people.' And some of the royal ladies were painfully shy.

Queen Victoria had ordered a 'white funeral' in her will, having got the idea from Lord Tennyson. She certainly had a white memorial service in Ottawa, where everything was in deep, shining snow. 'A most glorious day', wrote Louisa, 'real Queen's weather to the last . . . such a reverent impressive service – really as nice as could be. We got back to the House at 2. We skated in the afternoon.'

Over in England, the *Alberta* had carried the Queen's coffin to Portsmouth from the Isle of Wight, against a backcloth of royal sunset. An official ticket had been sent to Louisa for the funeral at Windsor, but of course she could not use it. Nevertheless, she, like everybody else, realized that a whole era had come to an end with this historic funeral. She could afterwards follow it step by step in her mind's eye. She could see her friend Lady Lytton travelling with the coffin from Portsmouth to London, the blinds of the train drawn and people kneeling in the fields as it glided past. She could watch the coffin being carried on a gun-carriage to Paddington station, along a route hung with white and purple instead of the conventional black. She could see her cousin Fritz Ponsonby handling the crisis caused when the horses, waiting at Windsor to draw the gun-carriage up the Long Walk, suddenly broke the traces; and Prince Louis of Battenberg telling Fritz to use his naval ratings to haul the gun-carriage instead, which he did. She could imagine the new courtiers mingling with the old and perhaps disagreeing, as they did. Above all she knew that the mysterious 'hush' at Windsor which pervaded Queen Victoria's last years would be broken. There would be normal talk and laughter. But would Louisa be there to hear it?

Louisa's last 'waiting' to Queen Victoria, 1 to 11 December 1900, was at Windsor.

Windsor Castle.

Benjamin Constant's visionary portrait of the Queen.
She was delighted by it.

The death of Prince 'Christle' in
South Africa had cast a pall of
gloom over the Court.

A last royal family group. Princess Louise reads to the Queen
with Princess Beatrice, Princess Thora and the Battenberg children.

Mary Hughes, a fellow
Lady in Waiting.

Frogmore Cottage, designed by Prince Albert. The Queen liked
to stop there on her visits to the Mausoleum.

Dorothy Vivian, soon to
become a Maid of Honour.

Dorothy Vivian

Aline Majendie

Mary F. Hughes

The Long Walk at Windsor. Louisa took
her last drive with the Queen on 6 December.

Aline Majendie.

Randall Davidson, the Bishop of
Winchester. He was to attend
the Queen on her deathbed.

Lady Churchill. Her death on Christmas Day 1900
was a final blow to the Queen.

Water-colour of Windsor Castle
painted for Louisa by Aline Majendie.

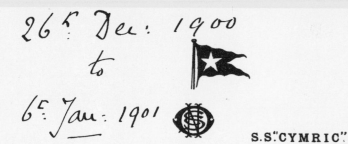

26ᵗʰ Dec: 1900
to
6ᵗʰ Jan: 1901

S.S. "CYMRIC"

The Countess of Antrim and Viscount Dunluce were among the passengers who left Liverpool by the White Star liner *Cymric* for New York.

S.S. "CYMRIC"

A HAPPY NEW YEAR
JANUARY 1, 1901

FRUIT
OATMEAL PORRIDGE   HOMINY
PLAICE   YARMOUTH BLOATERS
KEDGEREE   BROILED SALT MACKEREL
BROILED SIRLOIN STEAK & STEWED TOMATOES
CALVES LIVER & WILTSHIRE BACON
MUTTON CHOPS TO ORDER
IRISH STEW
MINCED CHICKEN & POACHED EGGS
PORK CHOPS
SCRAMBLED EGGS WITH CHEESE
(OMELETTES)
PLAIN, ECLARTE, BOLOGNA, SAVOURY & SWEET
BOILED, & FRIED EGGS
BROILED CUMBERLAND HAM & BACON
SARATOGA CHIP & SAUTÉ POTATOES
BUCKWHEAT CAKES
VIENNA & GRAHAM ROLLS
INDIAN CORN BREAD   SCONES
MUSTARD & CRESS
JAM   HONEY   MARMALADE

Menu for New Year's dinner.
'Luckily a calm evening', wrote Louisa.

Louisa on arrival in New York aboard S.S. *Cymric*.

Photographs taken by Louisa on her departure for Canada.

ABSTRACT of LOG

S. S. "CYMRIC." COMMANDER H. ST. G. LINDSAY R. N. R.

LIVERPOOL TO NEW YORK
PASSED DAUNTS ROCK L. V, 11·56, A. M. DECEMBER 27TH, 1900.

DATE	DIST.	LAT.	LONG.	REMARKS
DEC, 28	170	51 13	12 39	HEAVY WLY. GALE, HIGH SEA
,, 29	302	51 17	20 41	STRONG VAR, WINDS, CONFUSED SEA
,, 30	280	50 43	28 03	,, WLY, ,, HEAD SEA
,, 31	252	49 58	34 32	MOD, WLY WINDS & SEA
JAN, 1	278	48 28	41 11	STRONG HEAD WINDS & SEAS
,, 2	302	46 20	47 58	,, VAR, ,, CONFUSED SEA
,, 3	320	44 25	55 00	,, WLY, ,, ,, HEAD SEA
,, 4	277	42 46	60 27	FRESH ,, GALE ,, ,, ,,
,, 5	301	41 08	67 04	STRONG ,, WINDS ,, ,, ,,
,, 6	302	TO SANDY HOOK L. V.		

2784 TOTAL DISTANCE

Log of the *Cymric*, sailing for Canada. 28 and 29 December were the only two days Louisa did not keep her diary!

A last message from the Queen, after Louisa's arrival in Ottawa.

Helen Hay.

"Poets are born,
not made.
That is why there
are so many of them!"

=

Ian Malcolm.

ASKING PRETTILY.
Mr. Ian Malcolm
(The O-don't-he-gloss-'em Crisp-'em).

Ian Malcolm.

A walk in the snow – Louisa and companions.

Winston Churchill and friends set off for a sleigh ride.

Pamela Plowden,
who had been unofficially
engaged to Winston Churchill.

Winston S. Churchill.

The young Winston Churchill.

A winter view of Government House, Ottawa.

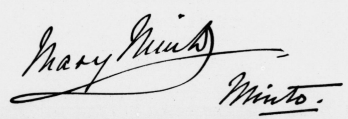

Louisa's sister
Mary, Lady Minto.

Lady Minto with her son, Viscount Melgund (Larry).

Violet and Esmond Elliot, the
Mintos' youngest children,
in sailor hats.

Ruby Elliot.

Lord Minto, Governor-General of Canada.

Two brothers – Larry Melgund and Esmond Elliot in a pantomime.

A small Elliot on skis.

A brisk ride in the snow.

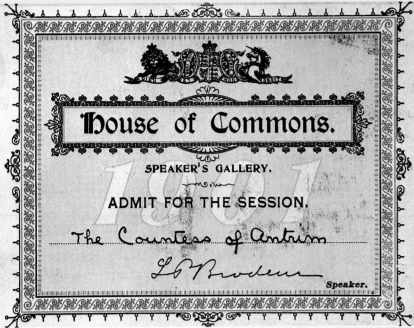

House of Commons.

SPEAKER'S GALLERY.

ADMIT FOR THE SESSION.

The Countess of Antrim

Speaker.

Louisa's pass to the Canadian House of Commons.

Wilfrid Laurier

Ian Malcolm
and Pamela Plowden.

Lt.-Colonel C.W. Drury,
commander of the Canadian
Field Artillery in South Africa,
home on leave.

Sir Wilfred Laurier, Prime Minister of Canada.
Louisa met him at dinner at Government House.

Two sisters – Louisa Antrim
and Mary Minto.

The Parliament building at Ottawa.

Avenue in Winter – photograph by Louisa.

The 'ice boat' – exhilarating transport for young passengers.

The Ice Palace.

Carnival programme collected by Louisa.

Ruby Elliot

Eileen Elliot

Eileen and Ruby Elliot and their dancing partners on the ice.

A talkative party sets out for an afternoon's skating.

Eileen Elliot and Larry on skis.

A line of skaters, cheerfully out of step, swings across the rink.

Bernard Howard (son of the Buzzard's sister Mabel), Angus McDonnell, Louisa's younger son, and a friend, in winter headgear.

Angus McDonnell and
Bernard Howard.

The 'small rink' at Ottawa.

Ice hockey. Louisa found it 'thrilling & exciting'.

Skating party.

The Canada Gazette

PUBLISHED BY AUTHORITY.

OTTAWA, WEDNESDAY, JANUARY 23, 1901.

DOMINION OF CANADA.

PUISSANCE DU CANADA.

HIS EXCELLENCY THE GOVERNOR GENERAL has received with deepest regret the news of the death of Her Majesty Queen Victoria, communicated to His Excellency in the following cable from the Right Honourable the Secretary of State for the Colonies :—

LONDON, January 22, 1901.

" Deeply regret to inform you that the Queen passed away at six thirty this evening."

(Signed) CHAMBERLAIN.

By Command,

HARRY GRAHAM,

Captain and A.D.C.,

Acting Governor General's Secretary.

Government House, January 23, 1901.

SON EXCELLENCE LE GOUVERNEUR GÉNÉRAL a reçu avec un profond regret la nouvelle de la mort de Sa Majesté la Reine Victoria, communiquée à Son Excellence dans le câblegramme suivant du Très honorable Secrétaire d'Etat pour les Colonies :—

LONDRES, 22 janvier 1901.

" Profond regret de vous informer que la Reine est morte à six trente ce soir."

Hôte

The official announcement of
Queen Victoria's death, 23 January 1901.

Memorial service in Christ Church Cathedral, Ottawa.

DEATH
OF
THE QUEEN.

Procession through Ottawa to the memorial service.
'Real Queen's weather to the last', wrote Louisa.

Death of the Queen:
Britannia mourns.

The Queen's last sea journey, from Osborne to Portsmouth harbour on the royal yacht *Alberta*.

The Mausoleum at Frogmore, where the Queen
was buried beside Prince Albert.

The Queen's coffin leaves Osborne, 1 February 1901.

63

Royal Chapel of St. George,
Windsor.

Saturday, the 2nd of February, 1901.

The Countess of Antrim

CHOIR.

Entrance South Door.

No Admittance after 12.45.

Louisa's pass for the Queen's funeral service.
She was still in Canada and unable to attend it.

The funeral procession
arrives at St. George's Chapel, Windsor.

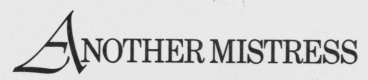

ANOTHER MISTRESS

MOUNTSTEWART
HATFIELD
AND MARLBOROUGH HOUSE.
DEATH OF THE
EMPRESS FREDERICK.
1901

It was with an agreeable shock that Louisa received an invitation from Queen Alexandra on 21 February to be her Lady in Waiting. 'A skating party in the aft. Such a beautiful day . . . I got the Queen's offer to be one of her ladies by cable wh: took me greatly by surprise.' There is no evidence that Louisa asked her Buzz for permission this time; or indeed that he made any objections, such as he had raised over his wife's appointment to Queen Victoria. 'Why should my wife have to wait on anyone?' he fumed – or such was the story told to his grandchildren – 'Like a damn servant!' It was by now obvious even to Buzz that his handsome Louisa and the Court needed one another. She accepted.

Louisa was not to come into waiting until 27 June. So there was time to fit in one or two of the houseparties that she so much loved. She boarded the *Teutonic* on 6 March ('a better lot of passengers than on the *Cymric*'), reaching Glenarm via London on 28 March ('Bill looking well & the house not as uncomfortable as I expected'). April saw her at historic Mountstewart in Ulster, where the redoubtable Lady Londonderry reigned. When Louisa came out in 1873, she had watched 'Nellie Talbot [as Lady Londonderry then was] fast growing up into startling arrogant beauty'. She had an affair with the wittiest of men, Harry Cust, which was exposed to Lord Londonderry by the jealous Lady de Grey; Lord Londonderry announced to his wife: 'Henceforth we do not speak.' Louisa had no dark areas and could speak to anyone, notably to Bill, who actually 'turned up' at Mountstewart one morning, and certainly, when occasion arose, to Mrs George Keppel, the King's clever and discreet mistress.

Louisa could not speak to Mrs Keppel at the next houseparty, however, for Hatfield House, where she arrived on 22 June, was a palace in which Alice Keppel was *not* received. What a family gathering this was! Apart from a few friends, like Nellie Londonderry and Louisa Antrim, all belonged in one way or another to the House of Cecil. For Lord Salisbury in old age had become bored with state functions, complaining that Hatfield was now too accessible to London: 'The facility of locomotion adds to the sorrows of human life in the shape of German Emperors and Princes of Naples.' (Kenneth Rose, *The Early Cecils*.) There were now no emperors or princes, their places being taken by the Cranbornes, Lord Hugh and Lord Robert Cecil, Lady Galloway (formerly a Cecil) and Lady Edward Cecil. Lord Milner, who was also present, lately ennobled and home on leave from governing the Cape, might almost be counted as an honorary Cecil, since Lady Edward Cecil had flirted with him while her husband was shut up in Mafeking, and was to marry him twenty years later.

Lord Salisbury had handed over foreign affairs to Lord Lansdowne in 1900, speaking with weary cynicism on the subject to Pom McDonnell, his Private Secretary. 'The work of the Foreign Office is very heavy and getting heavier. When I first became Foreign Secretary in 1878 there was no Egypt, except diplomatic – no West Africa, no Uganda and no Zanzibar, and no China to speak of.' His resignation from the premiership in 1902 was to free Pom for a new career at the Office of Works. The Buzzard would always introduce his brother as 'the only *successful* McDonnell'. But even Pom was not successful in controlling the untameable Buzzard. He once embarrassed Pom on a conducted tour of Hampton Court by leaping into Charles II's bed.

Queen Alexandra was also as flighty as a bird in her own way, though she possessed qualities that Louisa greatly admired and that marched well with her own character. The Queen's exquisite clothes struck an answering chord in the *grande dame* who bought her dresses at Paquin. No less did Louisa admire her kindness, sense of fun and showmanship. Alexandra's girlhood at Schloss Rumpenheim, where she was allowed to romp her way to maturity, was matched by Louisa's own 'wild and unruly' youth. (Looking back, Louisa was to write, 'I realize we had much more liberty than [most] children of our day . . . "Don't" was a word we hardly ever heard'). The Queen's showmanship became conspicuous the moment she was asked when full mourning had to stop. Could her Court drop the black dresses and jet beads for a grand function that happened to coincide with the last official day? Refusing to give a ruling ('such questions bore me intensely'), Alexandra guessed that her ladies would stick cautiously to black, as indeed they did, while she herself appeared in stunning white, gleaming with jewels, like a solitary star in the night sky. Louisa took a considerable interest in her own black garments, writing towards the end of her first waiting (2 July) 'I went early to Nina [Balfour] who Kodacked me in my "weeds".'

Louisa's old friends at Court had been thrown into a state of shock at the changes made by King Edward. 'Get this morgue cleaned up', he commanded, speaking of Buckingham Palace. The changes included turning Queen Victoria's daughters out of their apartments at Windsor, and also persuading Queen Alexandra to quit Marlborough House, to which, in the words of James Pope-Hennessy, 'she clung like a limpet'. It was in the garden of Marlborough House that she presented badges to 770 members of 'Queen Alexandra's' nurses on 3 July. Though at once obstinate and volatile, Alexandra was capable of at least one sustained interest – nursing. Dressed in black *crépon* for the occasion, with a pearl and diamond necklace, she looked, as Margot Asquith was later to write, 'dazzlingly beautiful . . . making every other woman look common beside her'. Louisa, who was actually beside her, certainly did not look common. In fact she had the style of beauty that Alexandra specially liked in her ladies: she was tall, which emphasized the Queen's own fragility. Louisa's account of this event, however, was not enthusiastic: 'lunched at Marlborough Hse. after wh. there was a function for nurses – about 1000 trooping past to be decorated – I got away at 5.' This function of course meant long hours of standing, which Louisa hated. But one advantage of the new Court was that bridge could be played after dinner, while non-players (to borrow Lord Esher's emphasis) '*sit* and talk'.

The old order finally passed away in August, when Queen Victoria's hapless daughter Vicky, mother of the Kaiser, died of spinal cancer at Kronberg. She had secretly instructed Fritz Ponsonby to smuggle out her correspondence with Queen Victoria lest it fall into the Kaiser's hands. Fritz succeeded (though he afterwards exaggerated the 'thriller' aspect of his exploit, as Vicky's granddaughter has since shown in her book *The Kaiser's Daughter*, 1977). Soon afterwards, Fritz went to fight in South Africa, a release that Queen Victoria had always denied him. Louisa thus lost a cousin and ally at Court to whom she was devoted. But the loss was only temporary, for yet another feature of the new order was to be Peace.

WHEREAS it has pleased Almighty God to call to His Mercy our late Sovereign Lady Queen *Victoria*, of Blessed and Glorious Memory, by whose Decease the Imperial Crown of the United Kingdom of *Great Britain* and *Ireland* is solely and rightfully come to the High and Mighty Prince *Albert Edward*; We, therefore, the Lords Spiritual and Temporal of this Realm, being here assisted with these of Her late Majesty's Privy Council, with Numbers of other Principal Gentlemen of Quality, with the Lord Mayor, Aldermen, and Citizens of *London*, do now hereby, with one Voice and Consent of Tongue and Heart, publish and proclaim, That the High and Mighty Prince, *Albert Edward*, is now, by the Death of our late Sovereign of Happy Memory, become our only lawful and rightful Liege Lord *Edward* the Seventh by the Grace of God, King of the United Kingdom of *Great Britain* and *Ireland*, Defender of the Faith, Emperor of *India*: To whom we do acknowledge all Faith and constant Obedience, with all hearty and humble Affection; beseeching God, by whom Kings and Queens do reign, to bless the Royal Prince *Edward* the Seventh with long and happy Years to reign over us.

Given at the Court at *St. James's*, this Twenty-third day of *January*, in the Year of our Lord, One thousand nine hundred and one.

GEORGE	Ridley	Rowton	H. D. Davies, Alderman
ARTHUR	H. Campbell-Bannerman	Herbert Maxwell	Alfred J. Newton. late Lord Mayor
GEORGE	G. Shaw-Lefevre	Charles Stuart-Wortley	John C. Bell, Alderman
CHRISTIAN, Pr. Schleswig-Holstein	Fred. Milner	Evelyn Ashley	H. George Smallman, Alderman
	John E. Gorst	James Bryce	G. Prior Goldney, City Remembrancer
F. Cantuar.	A. Graham Murray	Henry H. Fowler	Joseph C. Dimsdale
Halsbury, C.	C. Robert Spencer	R. Henn Collins	Marcus Samuel
Devonshire	Ripon	Colville of Culross	J. T. Ritchie
Salisbury	Goschen	Willelm. Ebor.	G. Wyatt Truscott, Alderman
Norfolk. E. M.	H. H. Asquith	C. Seale-Hayne	Saml. Green
Portland	Morris and Killanin	James Lowther	Forrest Fulton, Recorder
Pembroke and Montgomery	John Rigby	Edmond R. Wodehouse	G. Faudel-Phillips, Alderman City of London
Clarendon	Pirbright	Ford North	John Pound. Alderman City of London
Charles T. Ritchie	W. Hart Dyke	Horace Rumbold	John Knill. Alderman
J. Chamberlain	Richard Temple	Hertford	T. Vezey Strong, Alderman
Northumberland	Selborne	T. F. Halsey	Thos. Boor Crosby, Alderman
Cadogan	Arthur James Balfour	Carrington. Joint Hered. Lord Great Chamberlain	W Vaughan Morgan, Alderman and Sheriff
Fife.	John H. Kennaway	Jesse Collings	Joseph Lawrence, Sheriff
M. E. Hicks-Beach	W. E. H. Lecky.	Brampton	W. J. R. Cotton, Chamberlain
Ashbourne	Robert Montagu	Yarborough	John B. Monckton, Town Clerk
St. John Brodrick	Roland Vaughan Williams	S. Ponsonby-Fane	F. A. Bosanquet, Common Serjeant
Knutsford	Robert Romer	A. W. FitzRoy	Homewood Crawford, City Solicitor
Balfour o Burleigh	A. H. D. Acland	J. H. Harrison	Thos. Vaughan-Roderick, Secondary of London
George Hamilton	W. V. Harcourt	E. S. Hope	E. A. Baylis, Comptroller
Lansdowne	F. H. Jeune	W. R. Walkes	J. D. Langton, Under Sheriff
Walter H. Long	Leonard H. Courtney	Charles Dalrymple Hay	Thos. H. Gardiner. Under Sheriff
Spencer	H. Drummond Wolff	Frank Green, Lord Mayor	William H. Weldon
Argyll	James Stirling	David Evans, Alderman	
Rosebery	Charles W. Dilke	W. P. Treloar, Alderman	
Alverstone	Stalbridge	J. Whittaker Ellis, Alderman	
A. Akers-Douglas	M. E. Grant Duff	Henry E. Knight, Alderman	
Chesterfield	R. Couch	Reginald Hanson, Alderman	
Cork and Orrery	John Morley	Joseph Savory, Alderman	
A. L. Smith	Rathmore	Walter Wilkin, Alderman	
Kintore	William Ellison-Macartney	Joseph Renals, Alderman	
	Hobhouse		

God save the King.

The official proclamation of King Edward VII's accession, 23 January 1901.

King Edward VII.

Queen Alexandra has been pleased to make the following appointments in her Majesty's Household: To be Mistress of the Robes—The Duchess of Buccleuch and Queensberry. To be Ladies of the Bedchamber—The Countess of Antrim, the Countess of Gosford, the Countess of Lytton, C.I., the Lady Suffield. To be Extra Ladies of the Bedchamber—The Countess of Macclesfield, the Dowager Countess of Morton. To be Women of the Bedchamber—the Hon. Mrs. Charles Hardinge, the Lady Emily Kingscote, Miss Charlotte Knollys, the Lady Alice Stanley. To be Maids of Honour—Miss Mary Dyke, the Hon. Sylvia Edwardes, the Hon. Dorothy Vivian, the Hon. Violet Vivian. To be Lord Chamberlain—Lord Colville of Culross, K.T., G.C.V.O. To be Vice-Chamberlain—The Earl of Gosford, K.P. To be Treasurer—Earl de Grey. To be Private Secretary—The Hon. Sidney Robert Greville, C.V.O., C.B. To be Equerry—Colonel John Fielden Brocklehurst, M.V.O.

Queen Alexandra.

List of Queen Alexandra's appointments. Only two were from Queen Victoria's staff.

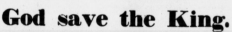

TELEGRAM Use this space for Continuation of Lengthy Addresses, OR INSTRUCTIONS TO MESSENGER.

To Lady Antrim
Ottawa
Canada

12/ Du
No. Check 32 govt

REC'D. No. 73 FROM Ino Y SENT BY RC'D BY Rm TIME 3 05 Pm Cable

Feb. 21 19—

From London.
It would give me the greatest pleasure if you would stay on as one of my ladies the same as you have been to our beloved Queen —

Alexandra

The telegram from Queen Alexandra to Louisa in Canada asking her to continue as Lady in Waiting. It took Louisa 'greatly by surprise'.

Mountstewart, the Londonderrys' house in County Down. It was famous for its beautiful gardens.

Lady Londonderry's bookplate. Louisa had commented on her 'startling arrogant beauty' when she was still only a girl. She became a passionate political campaigner.

Mountstewart,
Newtownards,
Co. Down.

Lady Helen Stewart, the Londonderrys' daughter.

Lady Londonderry, Louisa's contemporary and neighbour in Northern Ireland.

Group at Mountstewart. Back row, l. to r., Lady Helen Stewart, Lady Beatrice Pole-Carew, Sir Reginald Pole-Carew, Horace Plunkett; front row, Lord and Lady Londonderry, Lord Antrim, Louisa. This was one of the few houses that the Buzzard would visit.

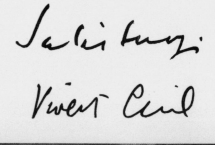

Salisbury.
Vincent Cecil

Louisa's next houseparty was at Hatfield House.

Lady Edward Cecil. She later married Lord Milner.

Lord Salisbury,
the Prime Minister.

Lady Londonderry.

Lord Salisbury detested official entertaining at Hatfield, and the party was made up of family and long-standing friends. Louisa described them as 'all very pleasant & nice'.

Schomberg (Pom) McDonnell, in the Buzzard's words 'the only *successful* McDonnell'.

Lord Salisbury on his tricycle. Specially laid tarmac on all the paths at Hatfield made the going smooth but he still needed two strong footmen to start him off.

One of the many panelled rooms at Hatfield.

Hugh Cecil

Alfred Lyttelton   Schomberg McDonnell

ONE THAT WAS LEFT.

TO DOWNING ST
AND WHITEHALL

LORD HUGH (left behind): *Please, mayn't I go too?*

The 'Hotel Cecil' by Carruthers Gould.
Five of Lord Salisbury's relatives were in the Cabinet.

Alfred Lyttelton.

Lord Milner. Back in triumph from governing the Cape,
he had been raised to the peerage in May.

Lady Cranborne.

Lord Cranborne (later fourth
Marquess of Salisbury).

The Marble Hall at Hatfield, with the Minstrels' Gallery. Lord Salisbury, who was a keen amateur scientist,
had installed electrical wiring in the house which sometimes set the panels smouldering.

Her Majesty Queen Alexandra, accompanied by her Royal Highness Princess Victoria, and the children of their Royal Highnesses the Duke and Duchess of Cornwall and York, arrived at Marlborough House from Sandringham this afternoon.

The suite in attendance consisted of the Lady Suffield, the Hon. Charlotte Knollys, and General the Right Hon. Sir Dighton Probyn.

The Countess of Antrim has succeeded the Lady Suffield as Lady-in-Waiting to her Majesty.

Louisa's first waiting on Queen Alexandra, 27 June to 4 July 1901. The King and Queen were still living at Marlborough House while Buckingham Palace was 'cleaned up'.

PROGRAMME OF MUSIC.

Fest Marsch in "Tannhäuser"	. . .	*Wagner*
Three Dances from the Music to "Nell Gwynne"		*German*
Selection from "Faust"	. . .	*Gounod*
(a.) Minuet	. . . .	*Boccherini*
(b.) Plantation Scene	. . .	*Lansing*
Overture . "William Tell"	.	*Rossini*
The Irish Patrol	. . . .	*Puerner*
Peer Gynt Suite No. 1	. . .	*Grieg*
Selection from "The Messenger Boy"	.	*Caryll*
La Danse Macabre	. . .	*St. Saëns*
Four Dances from "The Nutcracker"	.	*Tschaïkowsky*
Ice Dance in "La Vie pour le Czar"	. .	*Glinka*
Ballet Music from "La Reine de Saba"	.	*Gounod*

MARLBOROUGH HOUSE,	A. WILLIAMS, Mus. Bac. Oxon.
July 3rd, 1901.	*Bandmaster, Gren. Guards.*

Princess Victoria, Queen Alexandra's daughter. She made Louisa her confidante.

'Queen Alexandra's' nurses were presented with badges and certificates by Her Majesty on 3 July at Marlborough House. Louisa grew weary standing for hours at functions such as this. Above: The music played at the presentation.

As the President of all the Nurses in the British Empire, I am most anxious to express to every individual Nurse my heartfelt and grateful appreciation of their unselfish devotion and patriotism in ministering to, and relieving the suffering of, our brave and gallant soldiers and sailors who are fighting for their King and Country.

With the whole Nation I wish to convey to our invaluable Nurses the undying debt of gratitude we owe them.

Alexandra

THE ANGEL OF PITY

Queen Alexandra's message to the nurses of the British Empire.

The Empress Frederick of Germany died on 5 August 1901.

Mrs Fritz Ponsonby, the former Miss Victoria ('Ria') Kennard.

The Empress Frederick of Germany, Queen Victoria's daughter Vicky. Louisa's cousin Fritz Ponsonby accompanied King Edward to his sister's deathbed and secretly brought back, at her request, her correspondence with her mother.

Proclaiming the King's Coronation in London, 28 June.

Officers of the mounted infantry left for South Africa in November 1901. Captain Fritz Ponsonby was among them; he tried to enlist earlier but Queen Victoria would not let him go.

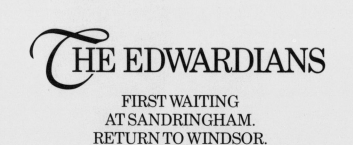

THE EDWARDIANS

FIRST WAITING
AT SANDRINGHAM.
RETURN TO WINDSOR.
'PEACE WITH HONOUR'.
1902

Louisa's first waiting at Sandringham was a new experience for her. In London she had lived at 39 Berkeley Street or 16 Hertford Street, performing her duties at Marlborough House by day and usually able to write in her diary, 'I got away at 4'. There had been something cosy about those Victorian waitings, like a girls' boarding-school, with few creature comforts and rather strict rules, but presided over by a beloved headmistress. Now she was under her new mistress's roof, and she knew it would not be like the old days. Christopher Hibbert, in his *Edward VII*, has said, 'there was a special *Gemütlichkeit* at Sandringham not to be found elsewhere'. But whatever its reputation for friendliness, Louisa was to make her first entry on 3 January with trepidation.

She reached Sandringham at six in winter darkness, its ornate gates and looming mass of nineteenth-century gables looking something like a glorified country club. 'Lady Farquhar & Lady Knollys in the room when I arrived', wrote Louisa, '– the Queen coming later – so kind but I was very shy.' Both ladies were wives of high officials, Sir Francis Knollys being the King's incomparable Private Secretary, and Lord Farquhar Master of the Queen's Household. As Pom McDonnell was soon to join the Office of Works, Louisa may have put in a timely word for her brother-in-law.

It is impossible not to feel that Louisa was homesick during this first visit. Though the house was luxurious compared with Queen Victoria's castles, it contained nothing much of interest except the splendid Goya tapestries in the dining-room, a present from the King of Spain. The weather was wretched and Louisa showed no sign of falling in love with the flat Norfolk countryside, unlike Queen Alexandra, who was pleasantly reminded of Denmark. '4 January. A hopelessly wet day – damp & muggy. All the same we went to luncheon with the shooters in a tent & walked back . . . going round by York Cottage to write names.' York Cottage was the adored home of the Prince of Wales, where five of his six children were born. Harold Nicolson, in his *George V*, calls it 'a glum little villa' smothered in dark rhododendrons, and Louisa probably thought the same. On Sunday she went twice to church, before and after breakfast ('very pretty & nicely done'), but in the afternoon her diary reverts to boredom ('we went round the gardens, stud etc., till I felt quite cold'). In the stud farm she must have seen the famous stallion Persimmon, who in 1896 had won the Derby for Edward. A painting of this event by S.Begg shows a sleek Prince of Wales leading in an even sleeker horse, while scores of top hats, if possible sleeker still, fly up into the air. This was not Louisa's mood at all, especially as the next day she had to inspect 'cart horses & bulls'. This was mitigated, however, by a call on Princess Maud, the Queen's daughter, and a walk with Sir Dighton Probyn, devoted member of the Household. He always referred to the Queen as the 'Blessed Lady'. Louisa's diary perks up when she is back in London and taking part in the procession at the Opening of Parliament. 'It interested me very much indeed – & it was a very pretty sight – home soon after 4. Pss. Thora & Marie Mallet coming in to tea – Pom dined & we had a very nice evening together.'

Louisa's return to Windsor on 20 January for various family ceremonies held the promise of enjoyment. 'We got to Windsor at 4. So nice to be in the dear old place again – the same old rooms – the Vivian twins are Mds. of Honour.' These lovely girls were called by the Queen 'my Heavenly Twins'. One of them, Dorothy, was to marry Douglas Haig, a name to be famous after the golden Edwardian age had been drowned in mud and blood. On the following day Louisa was kept busy 'running down' to receive the royal guests, who were arriving in strength for Queen Victoria's 'Mausoleum Day'. Louisa wrote: 'All the old Household came to the service at the Mausoleum at 12.15. We went down by 12 – it was most beautiful & impressive.' Though genuinely moved, Louisa did not hesitate to tell her grandchildren a wicked story attached to this solemn event. During the service a sparrow was trapped under the dome. 'Do you think that little bird could be Mama's spirit?' whispered a Princess to her neighbour. The whisper was repeated right down the line of Princesses until it reached Queen Alexandra. 'No, I do not think it could be Mama's spirit', she whispered back, 'or it would not have made a mess on Beatrice's bonnet.'

The confirmation of three of Queen Victoria's grandchildren took place next day. 'Mama's spirit' was surely among those present, but it failed to keep one of her former Ladies in Waiting quite up to the mark. It had been a hard day for Louisa: a 'very impressive' service at 12.30, a large luncheon, an afternoon painting away at candle-shades, lastly a large dinner – '& I was late wh: was rather awful'. It must have been the King whose disapproval was 'awful', since Queen Alexandra was nearly always late herself. From her carefree girlhood onwards she had been a model of unpunctuality. Nor did she attempt to eradicate this vice that maddened the King. Georgina Battiscombe, in her *Queen Alexandra*, describes an occasion when the Queen, having already kept him waiting for half an hour, turned to Sir Sidney Greville, one of his gentlemen, and remarked airily, 'Keep him waiting; it will do him good!' Another trait that the King regretted in his Consort was that of choosing her rooms in the royal palaces without consulting his needs. However, there was no hint of trouble when the Queen took Louisa up to see her newly decorated suite one day.

A series of parties at Windsor for members of the Government portended political activity. 'The Devonshires, Chamberlains & Mr Brodrick came down in time for dinner', wrote Louisa on 25 January. St.John Brodrick was Minister for War, but it was Joseph Chamberlain's presence that really augured a change in war policy. Once known as 'Radical Joe', he had since become a rampant imperialist at the Colonial Office. Lord Salisbury, the Prime Minister who lamented the very existence of most African countries, distrusted Chamberlain's enthusiasms, calling the South African conflict 'Joe's War'. Now at last a new force had arrived to press for peace. Edward VII thought it indecent that he should be crowned King of a country at war. His Royal Proclamation of last year had announced the date of his Coronation as 26 June 1902 – God willing. If the war were to end before the Coronation, the Government would have to move quickly.

Peace was indeed signed, on 31 May 1902: less than a month before the Coronation date. 'Blessed news of peace – wh: was known in London yest.' wrote Louisa from Glenarm on 2 June; 'it is a most unspeakable comfort.' She rushed back for the Thanksgiving Service at St. Paul's ('beautiful . . . most impressive'), but did not add that the Monarch looked monstrously overweight (his waist an incredible forty-eight inches) and dreadfully ill.

Louisa's first visit to Sandringham. The house was luxurious, and Queen Alexandra 'so kind', but Louisa felt 'very shy'.

Sandringham.
Norfolk.

Alexandra

December 8th 1902.

Edward R

Victoria.

The Princess of Wales with Princess Mary on her lap. The Wales's country home, York Cottage, was in the grounds of Sandringham – perhaps too close for comfort, for Princess May found frequent visits from her mother-in-law rather trying.

Princess Victoria ('Toria').

The Prince of Wales, the future King George V.

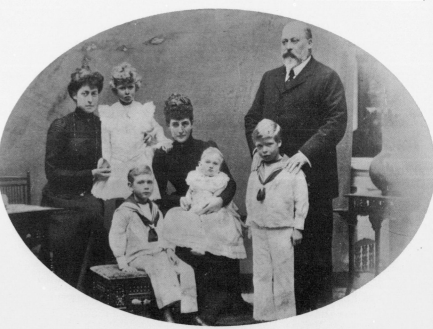

King Edward VII and his family. L. to r., Princess Victoria, Princess Mary, Prince Albert, Queen Alexandra with Prince Henry, Prince Edward, the King.

Maud
Charles
of Denmark

Princess Maud and her husband, Prince Charles of Denmark.
He became King of Norway in 1905.

THE CIGARETTE MAKER'S ROMANCE

Adapted by CHARLES HANNAN

From F. MARION CRAWFORD'S *Novel of that Name.*

COUNT SKARIATINE (*his Original Part*)
Mr. MARTIN HARVEY

ANTON SKARIATINE (*his Cousin, passing in Russia as "Count Skariatine"*) Mr. FRANK VERNON

CHRISTIAN - - - Mr. MICHAEL SHERBROOKE

DUMNOFF } Workers in the } Mr S. B. BRERETON

SCHMIDT } Cigarette Factory } Mr. CHARLES LANDER

HEINZ } } Mr. JOHN ALEXANDER

IKMENIEFF (*a Lawyer*) - - Mr. A. B. IMESON

NICHOLAS (*Friend of Count Skariatine*)
Mr. PAUL BARRY

VIERA (*her original part*) } Workers in the Cigarette Factory { Miss DE SILVA

ANNA } { Miss AMY COLERIDGE

AKULINA (*Mistress of the Factory*) Mrs. FREDERICK POWELL

AUGUSTA (*a Servant*) - - Miss B. ELDER

SYNOPSIS OF SCENERY.

Act 1.

SCENE ... ... The Cigarette Shop in Munich
(*Morning.*)

...

Act 2.

SCENE ... ... The Count's Lodgings at Schmidt's
(*Night.*)

Act 3.

SCENE ... ... The Cigarette Shop
(*The Next Day.*)

PERIOD, 1850.

"There is a greater thing than riches upon earth—with it the poor man is wealthy, without it the rich man is poor—beggars may possess it ; it is not to be bought by kings—the greatest thing in all the world——"

Theatricals brightened up Louisa's last evening at Sandringham.

SANDRINGHAM STUD.

1902.

STALLIONS.

AT THE STUD FARM, SANDRINGHAM.

NAME.		SIRE.	DAM.
PERSIMMON	1893	St. Simon Hampton	Perdita II. Hermione
DIAMOND JUBILEE	1897	St. Simon Hampton	Perdita II. Hermione

AT THE HEATH STUD FARM, NEWMARKET.

NAME.		SIRE.	DAM.
FLORIZEL II.	1891	St. Simon Hampton	Perdita II. Hermione

**All applications to be made to
LORD MARCUS BERESFORD,
32, St. James's Street, London**

A tour of the Sandringham Stud, obligatory for guests, was not much enjoyed by Louisa, who felt cold and tired.

The dining-room at Sandringham, hung with Goya tapestries given by the King of Spain.

Countess of Antrim.—Lady Antrim, who is lady-in-waiting to the Queen, was also lady-in-waiting to the late Queen, but she was one of Queen Victoria's later appointments. She owed her original selection to the favour in which Queen Victoria had held her father, General Charles Grey, who was for many years private secretary to the late Prince Consort and afterwards held the same office to the late Queen. When it became necessary to choose which of Queen Victoria's ladies-in-waiting should be continued in office the choice naturally fell on Lady Antrim, not only because of her obvious claims through her father but also because her youth recommended her to the younger Court. She is quite the handsomest and most elegant of the ladies-in-waiting and has a good deal of musical talent.

A complimentary description of Louisa.

Sir Francis Knollys, the King's Private Secretary.

Sir Dighton Probyn, Keeper of the Privy Purse.

The ballroom. On Twelfth Night there was a party here for staff and tenants, with presents round a towering Christmas tree.

Mrs George Keppel, the King's 'friend'. She was known to Louisa as 'La Favorita'.

The Marquess de Soveral, the Portuguese Ambassador and one of the King's wittiest and closest friends. He was nicknamed the 'Blue Monkey'.

Lady Sarah Wilson, sister of Lord Randolph Churchill.

GREAT EASTERN RAILWAY

TIME TABLE

OF THE

SPECIAL TRAIN

CONVEYING

THEIR MAJESTIES

The King and Queen

FROM

WOLFERTON TO ST. PANCRAS.

On Monday, 13th January, 1902.

			P.M.
WOLFERTON	... ...	DEP.	1 35
LYNN	... ...	ARR.	1.46
		DEP.	1.48
ELY	... ...	PASS	2.25
CAMBRIDGE	... ...	PASS	2 44
ST PANCRAS	... ...	ARR.	4. 0

H. G. DRURY, Superintendent of the Line.

Office of the Superintendent of the Line, Liverpool Street Station, 11th January, 1902.

The 'special' from Sandringham. 'A most easy journey' for Louisa, compared with those from Balmoral.

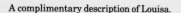

A great gathering at Windsor of Queen Victoria's family commemorated her death.
'Our day was spent running down to receive them', wrote Louisa.

Princess Margaret of Connaught.

The Duke and Duchess of Connaught.

Princess Louise (top) and
Princess Christian (Helena),
Queen Victoria's daughters.

Address.
—
Anthem.
Sir Walter Parratt.

*The Lord remember all thy offerings; and accept thy
burnt sacrifice. Grant thee thy heart's desire: and fulfil
all thy mind."—Ps. xx.*

SHE hath her heart's desire!
  She hath her joy!
Joy that no time can tire,
  Nor care destroy.

Now in the world of light—
  So near, so far—
Above her burns the bright
  And morning Star.

Here by the stroke of Love
  Her love was rent:
Now are they one above,
  In deep content.

Giver of Love and Strength,
  Of Life and Rest,
Lord, make us blest at length
  As she is blest.

A. C. Benson.

The Anthem at the memorial service.

*The Lord Steward
has been commanded by The King and Queen
to invite*

The Countess of Antrim

*to a Memorial Service at the Royal Mausoleum
Frogmore, on Wednesday 22nd January at 12 o'Clock.*

*Ladies and Gentlemen
Morning Dress.
Deep Mourning.*

Windsor Castle.
13th January 1902.

See other side.

Invitation to Louisa to attend the memorial service
on the anniversary of Queen Victoria's death.

The Royal Mausoleum, Frogmore.

Many of the royal family remained at Windsor for the confirmation
of three of Queen Victoria's grandchildren.

Princess Patsy of Connaught.
She became Lady Patricia
Ramsay.

Bishop Randall Davidson,
who conducted the service.

Confirmation service for Princess Ena (Victoria Eugenia)
and Prince Drino (Alexander) of Battenberg and
Princess Patsy (Patricia) of Connaught.

♔

WINDSOR CASTLE

Beatrice
Jan: 23rd. 1902.

Victoria Eugénie
of Battenberg.

Leopold of Battenberg.

Princess Beatrice and her four children. L. to r., Princess Ena, Prince Maurice, Prince Leopold
and Prince Drino. Louisa had known them since they were very small, and used to tell them stories at Balmoral.

Formal gardens at Windsor Castle.

Violet and Dorothy Vivian, Maids of Honour,
Queen Alexandra's 'Heavenly Twins'.

The Edward VI statue at Windsor.

King Edward's staff. From top,
Lord Churchill, Lord Pembroke
and Lord Clarendon.

Band of His Majesty's Scots Guards.

PROGRAMME.

EAST TERRACE, WINDSOR CASTLE.

JANUARY 26TH.

1. OVERTURE ...."Oberon" .... *Weber*

2. SUITE from the Incidental Music "Peer Gynt" .*Grieg*
   (Morning) (a) Death of the Ase. (b) Anitra's Dance. (c) Dance of Imps
   in the Halls of the Mountain King.

3. SONG ...."Serenade" ....*Schubert*

4. OVERTURE ...."Solenelle, 1812" ....*Tschaikowsky*

5. INTRODUCTION to III. Act "Lohengrin" .... *Wagner*

"God Save the King."

F. W. WOOD,
CONDUCTOR.

Sunday afternoon concert
on the terrace at Windsor.

The Red Drawing-room at Windsor, now used after dinner
instead of Queen Victoria's dreaded Corridor.

Government visitors came to 'dine and sleep' at Windsor later in the week.

The Duke of Devonshire, President of the Council.

The Duchess of Devonshire. Previously Duchess of Manchester, she was known as the 'double duchess'.

The White Drawing-room, also brought back into use by King Edward. He was slowly overhauling the castle.

Lord Esher, by 'Spy'. As head of the Ministry of Works he was in charge of the redecoration of the palaces.

Joseph Chamberlain, Colonial Secretary.

Mrs Joseph Chamberlain.

J. Chamberlain
Jan. 27. 02

Mary E. Chamberlain

PEACE AND HONOUR.

PEACE: *Thank you, Lord Kitchener. I knew you would be a good friend to me.*

The end of the Boer War, 31 May 1902. 'Blessed news of peace', wrote Louisa.

THE END OF THE WAR.

Its Cost in Men and Money.

The great Boer War, which began October 11, 1899, and lasted till May 31, 1902, has cost Britain 27,732 men and more than £200,000,000

ST. PAUL'S CATHEDRAL

SERVICE OF THANKSGIVING FOR PEACE

SUNDAY, JUNE 8th, 1902, at 10.30 a.m.

ADMIT TO SEAT UNDER DOME.

Enter by South Door.

To be seated by 10 a.m. at latest.

SOUVENIR PROGRAMME.

PEACE

Thanksgiving Service

AT

St. Paul's Cathedral.

ATTENDED BY THE

King & Queen & Royal Family,

ON

SUNDAY, JUNE 8th, 1902.

The thanksgiving service at St. Paul's, 8 June 1902.

The King and Queen on their way to the thanksgiving service.

CROWNS AND CORONETS

THE CORONATION
OF KING EDWARD VII
AND QUEEN ALEXANDRA.
1902

So absorbed was Louisa by the Coronation that she wrote a separate account of it on twelve sheets of lined paper. It was much franker than her usual diary.

Hardly anyone, even at Court, knew how sick the King was. And so Louisa's pre-Coronation diary concentrated entirely on her own preparations for the great day. With her sister Mary Minto she shopped hectically in Paris, 'did' Versailles, the Trianon and Petit Trianon in half a day, saw *Cyrano*, and visited the divine Sarah Bernhardt 'between acts!'. Back in London, a tooth extraction and still more dress fittings, from which she 'crawled back', culminated in a 'huge luncheon in an enormous tent' on 23 June, for the hordes of 'foreigners' who had poured into London. This was followed immediately by a Coronation rehearsal in Westminster Abbey – 'a great confusion'. It was only in describing the subsequent 'huge dinner' of 23 June that Louisa's diary gave the first hint of alarm.

Queen Alexandra had to receive the guests afterwards, alone – 'the King not so well'. Next day London was thrown into a confusion worse than that of the Abbey rehearsal on hearing the news that 'the King had had an operation and could not have the Coronation'. Louisa recorded 'consternation everywhere & appalling gloom – people were simply dumb . . . but so far all goes well – which is a mercy'.

The King in fact had undergone a successful emergency operation for appendicitis that he had courageously tried to ignore until the Coronation was over. 'I will go to the Abbey even if it kills me', he kept saying; and kill him it very nearly did. His Queen, with her vivid interest in nursing, had intended to watch the operation, but was asked to leave by the surgeon, already in rubber apron. Vast quantities of food, which had been prepared for the now departing royalties, were given away to the poor. Giles St. Aubyn, in his *Edward VII*, wonders whether they did not find the sole in oyster and prawn sauce, or the snipe stuffed with foie gras, 'a trifle rich for their taste'.

Perhaps, however, they said gratefully, 'It's an ill wind that blows nobody any good'. Certainly it did the King good to rest and diet for six weeks. Eight inches were removed from his waistline. Louisa thought he still looked 'pale & tired', but he was evidently made extremely happy by his tremendous reception at the Coronation, held at last on 9 August. The fact that the peers in the final rehearsal, wrote Louisa, had been 'partly in robes, partly in mufti & wholly ridiculous', did not prepare her for the 'magnificence & impressiveness of the real service'.

On the great day she was woken at 4.30 a.m. by the booming of cannon. Her hairdresser came at 7.15 and took a good hour to fix the 'all-round tiara' she had borrowed from a relative, the Duchess of St. Albans. With the family necklace of her sister-in-law Mabel Howard, and some antique gold embroidery she had found at Glenarm to embellish her white and gold dress, she felt able to 'hold my own with the other ladies'. The Glenarm embroidery had been put away in 1812, probably by Anne Catherine, the 'Lady Antrim' remembered in rhyme for a 'terrible tantrum'. Louisa wondered if the embroidery 'could not have given an account of former coronations'. No account, however, could have rivalled the present splendour of velvet and ermine, cloth of gold and silver, diamonds and sapphires, rubies and emeralds. The pile of the blue carpet on which Louisa walked with her 'pair', Lady Gosford, behind the Queen, was so thick that it forced her Majesty to 'step high', and dragged the Ladies in Waiting back by their 'golden tails'.

There were a few other oddities, such as 'other coronations' must have surely witnessed. The Duchess of Buccleuch's coronet was for a time 'at a marvellous angle', the strawberry leaves facing backwards. Louisa noticed one Lady in Waiting 'whose white satin stomach preceded her by some yards'. The Princess of Wales, however, though also in the family way, looked lovely, 'not showing coming events in the least'. Nothing but sympathy was felt by Louisa for the Duchess of Devonshire, who tripped while pushing her way out and 'rolled over like a rabbit'. Lord Rolles had done the same thing at Queen Victoria's Coronation, but from decrepitude. On this occasion the most decrepit dignitary present was the Archbishop of Canterbury, whose trembling hands had to be guided by the King himself at the Crowning and prevented from putting on the crown back to front. Louisa had greatly admired her friend Nellie Londonderry's 'gorgeous jewels' and 'magnificent crown'. Alas, this crown, or rather coronet, was to spend several minutes down the lavatory before Nellie could retrieve it, crying for 'forceps!'. Such a disaster had been at least unlikely during previous coronations, owing to the dearth of conveniences.

The Duke of Norfolk, as Earl Marshal, earned Louisa's high marks for taking the Oath of Allegiance in a 'stentorian voice'. Nor did she bear him a grudge for having earlier prevented her and Mrs Charles Hardinge from exploring the nave, after escaping from the annexe where the ladies had to wait for hours before the ceremony began. 'Kindly return to your place', he said to them in a meaning way, looking *past* them rather than *at* them.

The Bishops were glorious in gold copes, especially the Bishop of London, who sat patiently reading a book of devotions throughout the whole waiting period. Louisa wrote, 'I never could have kept *my* attention fixed!' Mr Balfour seemed 'strangely undressed' in mere diplomatic uniform, among all those superb Garter Knights; while Miss Charlotte Knollys, the Queen's permanent lady, was distinctly over-dressed. She had piled on the hired crown, jewels, chains, necklaces and collar, 'till she really had a *faux* air of the Queen'. (Poor Charlotte was extremely plain. Sir Dighton Probyn, who wooed but never wed her, had once given her a bathroom entirely lined with mirrors, which pleased her mightily.)

Louisa's only sharp criticism was reserved for the so-called 'loose-box'. The Princesses were seated in the chancel, looking 'extremely well' with all their crowns on the edge of the box in front of them. 'Just over them', continued Louisa, 'was the "loose-box" – & well named it was – to me the one discordant note in the Abbey – for to see the row of lady friends in full magnificence did rather put my teeth on edge – La Favorita [Mrs Keppel] of course in the best place, Mrs Ronny Greville, Lady Sarah Wilson, Feo Sturt, Mrs Arthur Paget & that ilk. . . .'

Louisa's loyalty to the Queen her mistress was absolute. What matter if the King had to chivvy her before starting? 'My dear Alix, if you don't come immediately you won't be crowned Queen!' To Louisa she was a paragon of virtue and beauty. 'She made one rub one's eyes & think of fairy stories', wrote Louisa at the end of her splendid account; ' – & even then the half is not said.'

Right Trusty and Right Wellbeloved Cousin. We greet you well. Whereas the twenty sixth day of June next is appointed for the Solemnity of Our Royal Coronation.

These are to Will and Command you (all excuses set apart) to make your personal attendance on Us at the time abovementioned furnished and appointed, as to your Rank and Quality appertaineth, there to do and perform all such Services as shall be required and belong unto you. Whereof you are not to fail. And so We bid you most heartily farewell.

Given at Our Court at St James's this second day of June in the second year of Our Reign.

By His Majesty's Command

To Louisa Jane Countess of Antrim

Louisa's summons to King Edward's Coronation on 26 June 1902. Its postponement on 24 June plunged London into 'consternation and appalling gloom'.

Crown Prince Ferdinand of Roumania. The beautiful Princess Marie of Edinburgh had married him in preference to her cousin George, Duke of York.

Crown Princess Marie of Roumania. She stayed on for the Coronation in August, to London's delight, and became known as 'Marie Remained Here'.

Princess Alice of Battenberg, the future Princess Andrew of Greece and mother of Prince Philip.

Princess Hélène of France, Duchess of Aosta.

The Duke of Aosta.

Buckingham Palace, where the State Banquet to celebrate the Coronation was to be held.

THRONE

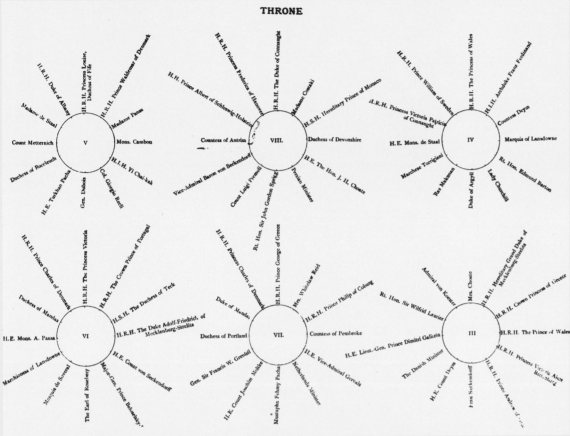

Plan of 'the banquet that might have been'. Louisa would have been escorted in by Prince Albert of Schleswig-Holstein.

Duke Charles of Coburg, son of Prince Leopold.

The Crown Prince of Denmark, Queen Alexandra's brother.

Princess Henry of Prussia.

The Grand Duke of Hesse. Louisa had attended his wedding to Princess Victoria. They were now divorced.

Prince Henry of Prussia. He represented his brother, the Kaiser. (The Crown Prince William was not allowed to come because of his 'unseemly frivolity' on his last visit to England.)

The Crown Prince and Princess of Greece. He was Queen Alexandra's nephew and she was the Kaiser's sister.

The Lord Steward has received The King and Queen's commands to invite The Countess of Antrim

to a State Banquet at Buckingham Palace, to celebrate Their Majesties' Coronation, on Tuesday the 24th of June at 8.30 o'Clock.

Full Dress.

Invitation to the State Banquet. It was cancelled the night before and the food given to the poor.

Indian Coronation Contingent

PARADE STATE.

Review by

H.R.H. The Prince of Wales,

HORSE GUARDS PARADE,

2nd July, 1902.

✳ ✳ ✳

Commanding Contingent :

LIEUT-COLONEL H. L. DAWSON, C.B.,

D.A.A.G. : CAPT. A. W. PENNINGTON,

D.A.Q.M.G. : CAPT. C. C. NEWNHAM.

Hampton Court,
2nd July, 1902.

Carriages arriving at Horse Guards Parade for the Review.

The Maharajah of Kolhapur.

The Maharajah
Kumar Madyot Tagore.

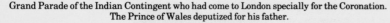
Grand Parade of the Indian Contingent who had come to London specially for the Coronation.
The Prince of Wales deputized for his father.

Lord George Hamilton,
Secretary of State for India.

Lady George Hamilton.

Their Majesties
The King, Emperor of India, and The Queen
have graciously signified their intention of being present

The Secretary of State & the Council of India
request the honour of the company of

The Earl — ss of Antrim

at the India Office, on Friday, July 4th at 10 o'clock.

Levée Dress   *R.S.V.P.*

Louisa's invitation to the India Office reception
given for the visiting Maharajahs.

The Maharajah Scindia.

The Review of the Indian Coronation Contingent.

Parade State of Colonial Contingents.

ALEXANDRA PARK CAMP.

Reviewed by GENERAL H.R.H. THE PRINCE OF WALES,

K.G., K.T., K.P., G.C.M.G., G.C.V.O.

Horse Guards Parade, 1st July, 1902.

FIELD-MARSHAL H.R.H. THE DUKE OF CONNAUGHT, K.G., K.T., K.P., Etc., Commanding.

MAJOR-GENERAL T. A. COOKE.
LIEUTENANT-COLONEL A. P. PENTON, R.G.A., *Chief Staff Officer.*
MAJOR C. J. ANSTRUTHER, H.P., 17TH LANCERS, A.D.C.

Head Quarter Staff, Alexandra Palace.

COLONY.	EUROPEAN.			NATIVE.			TOTAL.			COMMANDING OFFICER.	
	Officers	W.Os.	N.C.Os. and Men	Officers	W.Os.	N.C.Os. and Men	Officers	W.Os.	N.C.Os. and Men		
Head Quarter Staff ...	16	4	5	...	...	...	16	4	5	Major-General T. A. Cooke	
Australia ...	16	1	202	...	...	...	16	1	202	Lt.-Col.C.St.C.Cameron,C.B.	
Bermuda ...	1	...	5	...	...	16	1	...	21	Lieutenant C. S. Higgs	
British North Borneo ...	2	...	...	...	...	22	2	...	22	Captain C. H. Harington	
British South Africa (Rhodesia)	1	1	24	...	...	...	1	1	24	Major M. Straker	
Canada ...	26	3	628	...	...	...	26	3	628	Lieut.-Colonel H. M. Pellatt	
Cape Colony ...	4	4	142	...	...	...	4	4	142	Lieut.-Colonel R. F. Cantwell	
Ceylon ...	3	...	51	...	...	64	3	...	115	Major A. J. Farquharson	
Cyprus ...	1	1	12	...	...	...	1	1	12	Major A. E. Kershaw	
Fiji ...	1	...	...	...	1	19	1	1	19	Major A. B. Joske	
Sierra Leone and Gambia ...	1	...	...	...	...	23	1	...	23	Major J. E. C. Blakeney	
Sierra Leone Imperial Forces	1	...	...	...	...	26	1	...	26	Captain A. A. St. Hill	
Gold Coast...	1	1	...	...	...	32	1	1	32	Captain C. S. Haslewood	
Hong Kong ...	2	...	45	1	...	29	3	...	74	Major A. Chapman	
Jamaica ...	1	1	...	...	...	35	1	1	35	Captain C. M. Ogilvie	
Jamaica (Imperial) ...	1	...	...	...	...	39	1	...	39	Lieutenant A. E. Norton	
Lagos ...	1	...	...	...	...	25	1	...	25	Captain B. M. Read	
Malta ...	3	1	45	...	...	...	3	1	45	Major A. E. Mattei	
Natal ...	4	2	95	...	...	...	4	2	95	Lieut.-Colonel E. M. Greene	
New Zealand ...	6	1	126	...	...	30	6	1	156	Colonel T. W. Porter, C.B.	
North Nigeria ...	1	...	1	...	...	32	1	...	33	Lieutenant F. P. Crozier	
St. Lucia ...	...	...	...	...	...	3	...	...	3	Lieutenant A. E. Norton	
South Nigeria ...	1	1	...	...	...	49	1	1	49	Capt. W. J. Venour, D.S.O.	
Singapore ...	1	...	...	...	...	10	1	...	10	With Straits Settlements	
Straits Settlements ...	4	...	55	1	...	46	5	...	101	Lieut.-Col. Hon. A. Murray	
Trinidad ...	2	1	28	...	...	19	2	1	47	Major A. P. Lange	
Uganda (King's African Rifles) ...	3	1	...	1	...	29	3	1	29	Captain L. F. de V. Stokes	
Wei-hai-wei ...	1	...	1	1	...	14	1	...	15	Captain K. H. James	
Colonial Troops Ex. s.s. Bavarian	33	...	391	...	...	...	33	...	391		
TOTALS ...	136	23	1856	3	1	552	139	24	2408		

BY ORDER,

(Sd.) T. A. COOKE, *Major-General*

Order for the Parade State of Colonial Contingents.

Major His Highness the Maharajah of Bikanir.

Major Nawab Afsur Dowk Bahadur.

Sir Pertab Singh, Maharajah of Idar.

King Edward VII in Coronation robes. He was much thinner but, Louisa reported, 'still looking pale and tired'.

The Prince of Wales stood in for the King at several functions held for visiting foreign dignitaries. Here he meets the Indians.

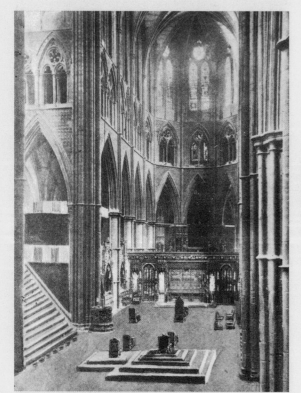

The nave of Westminster Abbey, showing the King's and Queen's thrones and Edward the Confessor's chair.

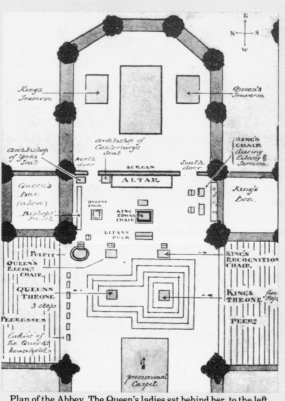

Plan of the Abbey. The Queen's ladies sat behind her, to the left.

Queen Alexandra. 'Her beauty made one rub one's eyes and think of fairy stories.'

The annexe to Westminster Abbey, where the procession formed. The sound of a minor explosion brought alarmed officials here after the service. They found Lord Esher picnicking amid popping champagne corks.

The Duchess of Sutherland.

The Duchess of Portland.

The Duchess of Montrose.

The Duchess of Marlborough. She and the three other duchesses pictured on this page held the Queen's canopy.

'An imaginary picture of Peeresses at the Coronation' which Louisa pasted into her album.

The Queen's Crowning; an artist's impression.

The Duchess of Buccleuch,
Mistress of the Robes.

The Duke of Norfolk,
the Earl Marshal.

Louisa in her Coronation robes. All the Queen's ladies
were in white and gold.

The Order of Procession through the Abbey.
Louisa was directly behind the Queen's pages.

Chaplains in Ordinary
Sub-Dean of the Chapels Royal

Rev. Canon Hervey — The Dean of Windsor

The Prebendaries of Westminster
Dean of Westminster
Pursuivants
Officers of the Orders of Knighthood
Heralds

Comptroller of the Household — Treasurer of the Household
Standard of Ireland — **Standard of Scotland**
Borne by the Right Hon. O'Conor Don — Borne by Henry Scrymgeour Wedderburn, Esq.
Standard of England — **Union Standard**
Borne by F. S. Dymoke, Esq. — Borne by the Duke of Wellington

The Vice-Chamberlain of the Household

The Keeper of the Crown Jewels, bearing on a cushion the two **Ruby Rings** and the **Sword**
The four Knights of the Order of the Garter appointed to hold the **Canopy** for the King's anointing

The Acting **Lord Chamberlain** — The **Lord Steward** of the Household
The Lord Privy Seal — The **Lord President** of the Council

Lord Chancellor of Ireland, attended by his Purse-bearer
Lord Archbishop of York
Lord High Chancellor, attended by his Purse-bearer
Lord Archbishop of Canterbury

Portcullis Pursuivant — Windsor Herald — Rouge Dragon

THE QUEEN'S REGALIA

The **Ivory Rod** with the **Dove** — The Lord Chamberlain of her — The **Sceptre** with the **Cross**
Borne by the Earl of Gosford — Majesty's household — Borne by Lord Harris
Two Sergeants-at-Arms — **Her Majesty's Crown** borne — Two Sergeants-at-Arms
by the Duke of Roxburghe

THE QUEEN

The Bishop of Oxford — in her Royal Robes, her Majesty's train — The Bishop of Norwich
borne by the Duchess of Buccleuch,
Mistress of the Robes, assisted by :—

Hon. Robert Palmer — Marquis of Stafford
Lord Claud Nigel Hamilton — Earl of Macclesfield
Hon. Edward Lascelles — Hon. Arthur Anson
Viscount Torrington — J. N. Bigge, Esq.

Ladies of the Bedchamber in Waiting
Countess of Gosford — Countess of Antrim
Lady Suffield — Countess of Lytton

Maids of Honour
Hon. Sylvia Edwardes — Hon. Mary Dyke
Hon. Violet Vivian — Hon. Dorothy Vivian

Women of the Bedchamber
Lady Emily Kingscote — Hon. Mrs. Charles Hardinge
Lady Alice Stanley — Hon. Charlotte Knollys

THE KING'S REGALIA

St. Edward's Staff — The **Sceptre** with the **Cross**
Borne by the Earl Carrington — Borne by the Duke of Argyll
A Golden Spur — **A Golden Spur**
Borne by the Earl of Loudoun — Borne by Lord Grey de Ruthyn

The Third Sword — Curtana — **The Second Sword**
Borne by Viscount Wolseley — Borne by the Duke of Grafton — Borne by Earl Roberts
Norroy King of Arms — **Ulster** King of Arms — **Lyon** King of Arms — **Clarenceux** King of Arms
The Lord Mayor of London — **Deputy Garter King of Arms** — **Gentleman Usher**
in his Robe, Collar, and Jewel, — in his Tabard and Collar, — of the
bearing the City Mace — carrying his Crown and Sceptre — **Black Rod**

The **Lord Great Chamberlain of England**
The High Constable of Ireland — The High Constable of Scotland
The Duke of Abercorn — The Earl of Erroll
The Lord High Steward of Ireland — The Lord High Steward of Scotland
The Earl of Shrewsbury with his White Staff — The Earl of Crawford, Deputy to his Royal Highness
the Duke of Rothesay (the Prince of Wales)

The Earl Marshal of — **The Sword of State** — **The Lord High Constable**
England, the Duke of Norfolk, — Borne by the Marquis — **of England**, the Duke of Fife,
with his Baton — of Londonderry — with his Staff

The Sceptre with the Dove — **St. Edward's Crown** — **The Orb**
borne by the Earl of Lucan — borne by the Duke of Marlborough — borne by the Duke of Somerset

The Patina — **The Bible** — **The Chalice**
Borne by the Bishop of Ely — Borne by the Bishop of London — Borne by the Bishop of Winchester

THE KING
The Bishop of Bath and Wells — in his Royal Crimson Robe of State, — The Bishop of Durham
wearing the Collar of the Garter,
on his head the Cap of State,
his Majesty's Train borne by :—

Ten Gentlemen-at-Arms — Earl of Portarlington — Marquis Conyngham — Ten Gentlemen-at-Arms
with their Standard- — Duke of Leinster — Earl of Caledon — with their Lieutenant
bearer and the — Lord Vernon — Lord Somers — and the Clerk of
Harbinger — and two Pages of Honour — the Cheque
H. E. Festing — Hon. V. A. Spencer
assisted by Lord Suffield, the Master of the Robes, his Coronet carried by a Page, and
followed by the Groom of the Robes

Admiral Sir Michael Culme-Seymour, — The Duke of Portland, — General Lord Chelmsford,
Vice-Admiral of the United Kingdom — Master of the Horse — Gold Stick in Waiting
The Duke of Buccleuch, Captain-General of the Royal Archer Guard of Scotland and Gold Stick of Scotland
Earl Waldegrave, — Lord Belper.
Captain of the Yeomen of the Guard — Captain of Hon. Corps of Gentlemen-at-Arms
The Lords in Waiting

Major-General A. Gaselee — Admiral Sir Edward Seymour — General Viscount Kitchener
Lord Knollys, — General the Right Hon. Sir D. M. Probyn,
Private Secretary to the King — Keeper of his Majesty's Privy Purse
Major-General Sir Arthur Ellis, Comptroller Lord Chamberlain's Department
Major-General Sir Henry Ewart, — Lieut.-Colonel Arthur Davidson, — Major-General Sir Stanley Clarke.
Crown Equerry — Equerry to the King — Equerry to the King
Colonel R. Ellison, — Colonel R. Hennell, D.S.O.,
Ensign of the Yeomen of the Guard — Lieutenant of the Yeomen of the Guard
Captain Houston French, — Major Hon. F. Colborne
Colonel F. B. de Sales la Terrière — Lieut.-Colonel C. D. Patterson
Exons of the Yeomen of the Guard — Exons of the Yeomen of the Guard
Major E. H. Elliot, Clerk of the Cheque to the Yeomen of the Guard
Twenty Yeomen of the Guard

Queen Alexandra with her pages. Her dress was made of gold-embroidered Indian gauze and her train lined with ermine.

The Coronation clergy: the Archbishops and Bench of Bishops.

The Archbishop of Canterbury. He tottered and nearly fell during the ceremony.

The Archbishop of York, who assisted at the ceremony.

The Queen paying homage to the King.

SOCIAL WHIRL

WASHINGTON, WINDSOR
AND ROYAL ASCOT.
1903

The Edwardian reign of pleasure was now well into its stride. Though Louisa felt worlds away from the fast set ('that ilk', as she had witheringly called it), the new age brought something of its pace into her own life. Houseparties followed one another in a mad kaleidoscope. During November alone she was to pack in visits to Beningbrough, Wynyard, Melchet, Panshanger, Temple Newsam and Aldenham. At times her 'Houghton & Gunn' diary became nothing but a string of glittering society names. (Houghton & Gunn themselves had changed little since the nineties, except to tell Louisa that their writing-paper was 'By Appointment to H.M. the King & Queen Alexandra' – and that Income Tax had gone up a penny in the pound since last year, to the grim figure of one shilling and threepence.)

It was at Aldenham that two of Louisa's closest American friends had recently settled: Jack and Jessie Morgan. Jack was the son of John Pierpont Morgan, banking paladin and founder of the great Pierpont Morgan library in New York. He was no beauty; indeed he has been called 'a bulbous-nosed banker' (in James Brough's astringent *Consuelo*); but President Cleveland once asked him to save the state, and he did so with a multi-million-dollar loan. Louisa had got to know the Morgans through her son-in-law Vivian Smith. A generation back, Vivian's uncle had established a connection with 'young Mr Pierpont Morgan', whose family owned an English estate at Roehampton near the Smiths. When asked to suggest partners for the London branch of Morgan's bank, Smith suggested his cousin Teddy Grenfell and nephew Vivian Smith. The partnership flourished. And for Louisa it was to open new doors not only at Aldenham but in America.

She made a flying visit to America (from Ottawa) in January. Though the train to Washington was very late she found the British Ambassador, Sir Michael Herbert, and his wife Belle waiting up for her. The next day Louisa's young relative, Hugo Baring, drove her around the city till tea-time at the embassy. 'The Herberts have made the Embassy quite lovely.' She tended to think any place lovely that was not Glenarm. 'We went in the Herberts' carriage', she continued, 'to see the library & then to luncheon at the White House wh: was most interesting.' The same cannot be said of Louisa's account of it. There is not a word about the abrasive personality of the President, Theodore Roosevelt, who was much admired in England. Louisa permitted herself no comment more audacious than, 'I liked both the President & Mrs Roosevelt very much'. After luncheon, 'We went to the Capitol & peeped into the Senate, Supreme Court & House of Representatives'. Who said the Americans were the only hustlers?

On 27 January Louisa left Washington at 10 for New York at 5, where 'Angus & I went to tea with Mrs Morgan'. The great J.P. Morgan himself gave her a spoof Permit to 'walk about the Earth'. If only she could continue doing so. . . . But after a 'most sumptuous repast' with Hugo Baring and a visit to the play, she had to board the SS *Celtic* for home. These huge liners were to bewitch the Edwardians as 'Jumbo' jets spellbind their descendants. The *Celtic*'s smoothness was 'really wonderful'. It enabled Louisa to recover from her whirlwind tour. 'We were on deck from 10 a.m. till 6.30 p.m. wh: must be wholesome.' She landed in high feather, only to find a sadly moulting Buzzard.

As in the fairy tale of *Beauty and the Beast*, the poor Beast had sickened while Beauty was spending her enchanted two months across the Atlantic. 'Glenarm. February 10. I arrived about 10.20. found poor Bill very no how & still weak & low – but getting on – talked to him all day. . . .' She got him to London in March, her grandchildren Rufus and Vere 'squeaking with joy' to see her again, and dressing up in her honour. (They were invited to a fancy-dress children's party at Buckingham Palace in June.) But Bill required medical attention. Sir Frederick Treves, who had operated on the King, persuaded the reluctant Antrims to spend much of April in Bath. Louisa escaped to a houseparty for a few days, only to be summoned back by telegram. 'Poor Bill so glad to see me his kidneys affected by flue. . . .' It was not until 18 April that they 'got the blessed permission to leave Bath'.

Meanwhile Louisa's Court life, when it functioned, was full of variety. One day she would be shown the Queen's new room at the Palace, on another, the painter Sir L. Alma-Tadema's studio, a dream of mosaics and marble. The season reached its climax with Royal Ascot and the Windsor houseparty. Louisa 'prowled around' the Van Dyck room on 17 June. On the next day she drove up the course in the royal cavalcade. Here she saw many major stars of the Edwardian era, all – for the present – scintillating in harmony. In the fourth carriage was Consuelo Duchess of Marlborough. Half a head taller than her husband, she had been forced at nineteen by her mother Alva Vanderbilt into a loveless marriage; it was dissolved two years later. Nellie Londonderry was her friend, and so was Louisa, to whom she gave a charming photograph of her two small sons Bert and Ivo. In the fifth carriage sat the vivacious Marquess de Soveral, the King's *alter ego* and the Court's 'Blue Monkey'. And in the sixth, with Louisa herself, sat Count Albert Mensdorff, the Austrian Ambassador whose duty it was to see, if possible, that Queen Alexandra and Mrs Keppel were not invited to the same parties.

Opposite their Majesties in the first carriage reposed the venerable Duke of Cambridge. He was odd-man-out in this Edwardian galaxy, and was to die the following year. With his passing, the old order made its positively last bow. As Queen Victoria's Commander-in-Chief, he had been an almost irremovable obstacle to army reform. At the same time he had gallantly married his actress-mistress and raised three soldier sons, the Fitzgeorges, despite royal opposition, behaving with great firmness and decorum.

Louisa revelled in the dazzling ball given on 19 June in the Waterloo Gallery, the first to be held there for half a century. 'So well done', wrote Louisa. Everything, that is, except Alice Keppel's gown. This was overdone. 'So awfully long', wrote Princess May (and no doubt loose) that it caught the spurs of Prince Adolphus ('Dolly') of Teck, toppling him and his partner Princess 'Toria' flat on their backs.

Charity was represented by Lady Maud Warrender's concert at the Albert Hall. Agriculture, in the shape of huge pedigree beasts at the Show, bored Louisa. Perhaps they reminded her too much of Bill's fat cattle. Her most unusual experience was to accompany their Majesties to Ibsen – in French, with the great Réjane. Not Ibsen's *Ghosts*, of course. Edwardian ladies avoided its theme of unmentionable hereditary disease. It was his *Doll's House* that they saw. There were great ladies all over Europe and America beginning to sympathize with women's longing to leave their dolls' houses.

Voyage to America, December 1902, on the *Oceanic*.

The hazards of an Atlantic crossing are present even on a luxury liner.
This cartoon is by Louisa's son Ducie (self-portrait to the right).

d. B. Herbert

Michael H. Herbert

The President and Mrs. Roosevelt yesterday entertained at luncheon Lady Minto, Lady Antrim, Secretary Hay, Secretary Root, Senator and Mrs. Lodge,
and Dr. Henry Van Dyke.

Sir Michael and Lady Herbert,
the British Ambassador and
his wife.

The British Ambassador and Lady Herbert entertained in honor of the Countess
of Minto, wife of the governor general of
Canada, who, with her sister, Lady Antrim, and her young daughter, Lady Elise
Elliot, is spending several days at the
embassy. To meet these distinguished
visitors were the Postmaster General and
Mrs. Payne, Senator Frye, Senator and
Mrs. Lodge, Senator and Mrs. Hale, Justice and Mrs. Holmes, the Danish Minister, Mr. and Mrs. Boardman, Miss
Boardman, Mr. and Mrs. William Eustis,
Mr. and Mrs. George B. McClellan, Miss
Hitchcock, daughter of the Secretary of
the Interior; Miss Warder, Capt. Guise,
aid-de-camp of Canada; Mr E. V. Mor

The visit to Washington. Louisa
and her sister Mary Minto
stayed at the British Embassy.

On her whirlwind tour of the city,
Louisa visited Washington's monument (above).

The White House. Louisa was entertained to luncheon by President Roosevelt.

The Capitol.

PERMIT

To allow the Bearer to walk about the Earth

John Pierpont Morgan.

Registered No. 8000976485546.

Souvenir from John Pierpont Morgan, the great collector and founder of the Morgan library in New York. His son Jack was a close friend of the Antrims.

President Theodore Roosevelt.
Louisa liked him 'very much'.

LAUNCH OF THE TWIN SCREW STEAMER "CELTIC"

April 4th 1901

QUEEN'S ISLAND, BELFAST

Louisa returned to England on the *Celtic*, the 'biggest ship in the world', which she had seen launched from the great shipyards in Belfast in 1901. The *Celtic* was outclassed by her sister ship, the ill-fated *Titanic*, in 1911.

Consuelo Marlborough. Marlborough

Above: The Duke of Marlborough. Left: The Duchess of Marlborough.

WINDSOR CASTLE

George 1903

The old Duke of Cambridge at Windsor.
The last of Queen Victoria's cousins, he died in March 1904, aged 85.

The Royal Box at Ascot,
at the height of the social season.

PROCESSION TO ASCOT.

JUNE 16th and 18th, 1903.

To leave Windsor Castle at 12.15 p.m.

FIRST CARRIAGE.

THE KING.
THE QUEEN.
H.R.H. THE PRINCE OF WALES.
H.R.H. THE DUKE OF CAMBRIDGE.

SECOND CARRIAGE.

H.R.H. THE PRINCESS OF WALES.
H.R.H. THE PRINCESS VICTORIA.
H.R.H. THE PRINCE CHRISTIAN OF SCHLESWIG-HOLSTEIN.
H.E. COUNT BENCKENDORFF.

THIRD CARRIAGE.

H.R.H. THE PRINCESS CHRISTIAN.
H.R.H. THE PRINCESS HENRY OF BATTENBERG.
H.H. THE PRINCESS VICTORIA OF SCHLESWIG-HOLSTEIN.
H.H. THE PRINCESS LOUISE OF SCHLESWIG-HOLSTEIN.

FOURTH CARRIAGE.

THE DUCHESS OF MARLBOROUGH.
THE COUNTESS BENCKENDORFF.
H.H. THE PRINCE ALBERT OF SCHLESWIG-HOLSTEIN.
THE DUKE OF PORTLAND.

FIFTH CARRIAGE.

THE DUCHESS OF PORTLAND.
THE COUNTESS OF DERBY.
THE DUKE OF MARLBOROUGH.
THE MARQUESS DE SOVERAL.

SIXTH CARRIAGE.

THE COUNTESS OF PEMBROKE AND MONTGOMERY.
THE COUNTESS OF ANTRIM.
COUNT ALBERT MENSDORFF-POUILLY.
H.E. COUNT SECKENDORFF.

Order of the procession from Windsor Castle to Ascot.

Members of the royal party at Ascot.

The royal procession up the course. Louisa noted 'clouds of beauties'.

The Marquess de Soveral,
one of the royal party at Ascot.

The Earl of Rosebery, a keen
racing man and winner of
several classic turf events.

The King and Queen leaving Windsor for London, 22 June.

THE KING'S CHAMPION DEVON BULL THE KING'S CHAMPION HEREFORD MR. HANDLEY'S CHAMPION SHORTHORN

CHAMPIONS AT THE ROYAL AGRICULTURAL SHOW.

THE CHAMPION BERKSHIRE LORD LLANGATTOCK'S CHAMPION SHIRE THE CHAMPION WHITE PIG

Exhibits at the Royal Agricultural Show.
'A long and tiring entertainment', wrote Louisa.

Verdi's *Otello*, sung by Alvarez. The Queen was a great opera-goer, and Louisa an enthusiastic companion.

The famous actress Madame Réjane played in Ibsen's *The Doll's House*, which delighted Louisa.

Souvenir Programme and Book of Words of Lady Maud Warrender's Grand Concert In Aid of the Union Jack Club at the Royal Albert Hall, Thursday Evening, June 25th, 1903 under the Direction of Mr. J. Henry Iles

The 'Union Jack' concert arranged by Lady Maud Warrender. Louisa embellished the programme with photographs of the performers.

At the Albert Hall last Thursday, Lady Maud Warrender gave a Grand Concert in aid of the Union Jack Club, at which the King and Queen were present, together with the Prince and Princess of Wales. The Choir of the Leeds Choral Union sang Sullivan's "God sent His Messenger, the Rain," from "The Golden Legend," with great vitality and purity of tone. Mr. Andrew Black sang "The Union Jack in Town" with immense verve; but it was a great mistake to have placed his song immediately after the choral singing, coming as this did to us with so enormous a volume of sound. Madame Clara Butt sang "The Lost Chord," accompanied by the Queen's Hall Orchestra and Grand Organ; it is a song which exactly suits her wonderful voice, and she interpreted it splendidly. Miss Marie Hall played the solo violin in the first Movement from Tschaïkowsky's Concerto for Violin and Orchestra, giving to it all the feeling and technical skill of which she is capable. Mr. Henry J. Wood conducted the Concerto, and also Tschaïkowsky's "1812," played with splendid effectiveness by the Queen's Hall Orchestra and Massed Bands. Madame Albani sang Bach-Gounod's "Ave Maria" with all her well-known skill, the violin obbligato being played by Miss Marie Hall. Altogether, the concert was remarkably interesting, and it assuredly drew a very large audience to the Albert Hall. COMMON CHORD.

Sybil's third child, Mary, dressed as Baby Bunting.

Sybil's second child, Vere, as 'a Van Dyck'.

Japanese 'daylight' fireworks raining toys at the Buckingham Palace party. Princes David (Edward VIII) and Bertie (George VI) squabbled over them and had to be forcibly separated.

BUCKINGHAM PALACE.

The Master of the Household

has received

Their Majesties commands

to invite

The Countess of Antrim.

to a Children's Party on

Saturday the 6th July 4 to 6.30 o'clock.

Children between   *Morning Dress.*
2 and 15 years of age.

Invitation to one of Princess Victoria's birthday parties at the Palace, an annual event much enjoyed by Louisa's grandchildren.

Sybil's eldest child, Rufus, as 'Bubbles'.

PROGRAMME OF MUSIC.

1. OVERTURE	..	"Haydée"	..	..*Auber*
2. CHANT SANS PAROLES	..	..	..*Tschaikowski*
3. VALSE BLEUE ..	..	..	..	..*Margis*
4. SELECTION	.."My Lady Molly"	..*Sidney Jones*
5. HUNGARIAN LOVE SONG	..	..	..*Klay*
6. SELECTION	"Blue Bell in Fairyland"	..*Slaughter*
7. SERENADE	"Quand tu Chantes"	..*Gounod*
8. VALSE ..	..	"Tout Passe"	..*Berger*
9. SUITE ..	"Three Quotations"	..*Sousa*
10. MORCEAU	"Les Cloches de St. Malo"	*Rimmer*
11. VALSE DES FLEURS ..	..	..*Tschaikowski*
12. FOUR DANCES IN "Merrie England"	.*German*

"GOD SAVE THE KING."

C. H. HASSELL,
BUCKINGHAM PALACE,   *Bandmaster Irish Guards.*
23rd June, 1903.

Programme of music played at the children's party by the band of the Irish Guards.

VISITORS OF STATE

MARRIAGE OF PRINCESS ALICE.
ROYAL VISIT TO IRELAND.
QUEEN AMÉLIE OF PORTUGAL.
1904

This year was going to be one of extreme royal splendour. The wedding of H.R.H. Princess Alice of Albany to H.R.H. Prince Alexander ('Alge') of Teck was a good start. So Louisa, it seems, saw fit to begin it with some severe penitential exercises in Ireland: doing accounts, organizing village treats for the 'children' and the 'R.C. children' (separately), and calling on old age pensioners – 'poor things some of them are so pathetic'. She left for England on 29 January, and the tone and tempo of her diary changed with a bang.

Bang was the word. For the first shots in the Russo-Japanese war coincided with the first foreign royalties' arrival at Windsor station. It gave a curiously staccato effect to Louisa's account. 'We received royalties [indigenous] & went to the S. Western [station] to receive the Queens [Queen Mother of the Netherlands and Queen of Würtemberg] who came with the Dss. of Albany [bride's mother] & bride. A large tea in red dg room & a large dinner in Esther Tapestry Room *so* pretty. Sitting in Van Dyck room – later we had to go to red dg room when royalties came & "mingled" – the foreigners mostly *very* plain. . First shot between Japan & Russia – Japs entering Port Arthur & torpedoing Russian ships.' One might have expected Louisa to see the War in terms of Royalties v. Foreigners, since the Russian Tsarina was Queen Alexandra's sister. But Russian aggression had been recommended by the Kaiser – that growing bugbear of British politics. The Court therefore was pro-Japanese.

The odd effect of guns going off in the background was maintained next day: 'a large tea in red dg room – & a big dinner in Waterloo Gallery with a most delightful concert afterwards. Clara Butt – Kennerley Rumford. . . . I went to supper with the artistes. News of Russian ships being sunk.'

It was rightly a popular wedding. Princess Alice's late father was Prince Leopold, Queen Victoria's clever but unlucky fourth son, a haemophiliac who died at thirty-one. Who could have guessed that his only daughter would be alive and alert in 1979, aged ninety-six? Perhaps her unruffled expression in her wedding photograph was a good sign. Calm was called for during a wedding when the Castle was fairly bursting with foreign royalties and their suites. From Tower to Tower – Lancaster, York, Victoria, Edward III's – German voices hailed one another with genial guttural greetings or sharp commands. Since Louisa was German-speaking, she sat between two Germans at the royal banquet before the wedding day.

The date of Princess Alice's wedding was the same as that of her grandmother, Queen Victoria: 10 February. Louisa wrote. 'Fine for a wonder – the wedding was about 12.45 really beautiful the breakfast in St. George's Hall very fine indeed for 200 guests – we got to our rooms to rest a bit at 3.30 then tea & a banquet in the evening for 100, again in St. George's Hall – the most beautiful thing I ever saw – standing about in tapestry room afterwards – everyone very tired but impressed.'

King Edward, the bride's uncle Bertie, behaved urbanely, despite a mistake by his military escort of the kind to make him livid. They failed to turn up in strength. He gave his niece only one piece of advice on her marriage. 'Wherever you may be, always remember to go to church on Sunday.' This surprised Alice, since Uncle Bertie's laxity as a young man had often worried his mother. Princess May looked forward to a happy future for her brother Alge with Alice, 'as she has been well & sensibly brought up'.

For Louisa, the day after the wedding ended in bathos, though it began well, with the entry 'Great departure [of foreigners] from the Castle'. After lunching and dining at Buckingham Palace, she 'went with the K & Q to the Gaiety – very stupid & vulgar'.

The royal visit to Ireland in April was the acme of elegance, as well as of pleasure. Louisa had suddenly received on 11 April another of those exciting 'wires' from the Duchess of Buccleuch, Mistress of the Robes, 'asking me to be in waiting on 19th wh: a little upsets my plans – however I must try to be ready'. But first there was an evening Presentation Court at the Palace, already an established feature of the new reign, replacing Queen Victoria's unglamorous afternoon Drawing Rooms – 'really very pretty & not long'.

On 25 April Louisa and all of them embarked at Holyhead on the new royal yacht, *Victoria & Albert*, 'the beauty of wh: cannot be described – nor its comfort'. It had been built in 1901 at enormous cost. 'We slipped across quite easily at 4 a.m.', wrote Louisa, no doubt remembering their tossing on Queen Victoria's old yacht four years before. What did the King remember of the past, when they attended Punchestown and Leopardstown races during their first days of the state visit? His mother's fears that he would be corrupted by Punchestown and so must not have a home in Ireland as his friends wished? Or, going further back, his first 'fall' with the actress Nellie Cliften at the Curragh? There was only one blot on 1904: the Corporation of Dublin voted by 43 to 38 against presenting a Loyal Address to their Majesties on arrival. Louisa's impression, however, was of popular ecstasy. The crowd was 'most enthusiastic' when the King laid the foundation stone of a College of Science, and there was 'a wonderful reception' at the play.

On 30 April they moved to Kilkenny Castle ('quite splendid, a magnificent situation'), where medieval walls, raised in an age of violence, now looked down on the stolid benevolence of royal faces lined up for a photograph. Endless processions, entraining and detraining on 2 May carried them from Waterford and pedigree cattle in the morning, to the Duke of Devonshire's romantic Lismore and Sir Ernest Cassell and Lady Sarah Wilson of 'that ilk' in the afternoon. If Louisa slept on the river side of the Castle, she would have woken to look straight down into the clear depths of the Blackwater far below. After exploring the Lismore country 'wh: beggars description – it is so beautiful', they returned to Kingstown Harbour on 4 May, for a 'musical send-off', with its optimistic finale '*Come back to Erin*' and '*Welcome Galore!*'

It might be thought that the King and Queen of Portugal's state visit to Windsor in November would have proved an anti-climax for Louisa. Far from it. She found Queen Amélie's personality enchanting; though the luxury and grandeur of Windsor may have adversely affected the character of that 'little man' her husband, sending him home with dangerous ideas. No one, fortunately, could foresee his forthcoming assassination. Louisa was more than happy to begin a lifelong friendship with Queen Amélie, signified by a flow of affectionate royal cards and letters – and 'a lovely bracelet'.

WINDSOR CASTLE.

THEIR MAJESTIES' GUESTS,

FROM

Monday, 8th February, to Thursday, 11th February, 1904.

The Marriage of Her Royal Highness Princess Alice of Albany.

Drawing-room at Windsor Castle.

THEIR MAJESTIES THE KING AND QUEEN OF WÜRTEMBERG	Rubens Room, Council Chamber, Queen's Closet, Picture Gallery, Van Dyck Room	Valet ....441, North Front Dresser ....434, North Front Dresser ....435, North Front Page ....522, North Front 2 Footmen ....412, Box Lobby	
HER MAJESTY THE QUEEN MOTHER OF THE NETHERLANDS.................	240, 243, 244, Lancaster Tower	Dresser ....169, Lancaster Tower Page ....63, Lancaster Tower Footman ....21, Lancaster Tower	
HIS ROYAL HIGHNESS THE DUKE OF SAXE-COBURG AND GOTHA	52, Victoria Tower	Valet ....54, Victoria Tower Jager ....21, Lancaster Tower	
HER ROYAL HIGHNESS PRINCESS LOUISE (DUCHESS OF FIFE) AND THE DUKE OF FIFE	233, 235, 236, 238, York Tower	Dresser ....147, York Tower Valet ....157, York Tower Footman ....17, York Tower	
THEIR ROYAL HIGHNESSES THE DUKE AND DUCHESS OF CONNAUGHT	303, 304, 305, Victoria Tower	Dresser ....612, Victoria Tower Dresser ....119, Clarence Tower Valet ....609, Victoria Tower 2 Footmen ....16, York Tower	
THEIR ROYAL HIGHNESSES THE DUCHESS OF ALBANY AND PRINCESS ALICE OF ALBANY	248, 250, 251, Lancaster Tower .... (Blue Rooms.)	2 Dressers ....171, Lancaster Tower Footman ....21, Lancaster Tower	
HIS ROYAL HIGHNESS PRINCE ARTHUR OF CONNAUGHT	128, Victoria Tower	Valet ....609, Victoria Tower	
THEIR ROYAL HIGHNESSES PRINCESSES MARGARET AND VICTORIA PATRICIA OF CONNAUGHT	121, 125, Victoria Tower ..	2 Dressers ....127, Victoria Tower Footman ....16, York Tower	
THEIR SERENE HIGHNESSES THE REIGNING PRINCE OF WALDECK-PYRMONT AND THE PRINCESS OF WALDECK-PYRMONT	255, 256, 257, 259, Edward 3rd's Tower	Dresser ....67, Edward 3rd's Tower Jager ....71, Edward 3rd's Tower	
PRINCESS HELEN OF WALDECK-PYRMONT	352, 353, Edward 3rd's Tower	Nurse ....Same rooms	
THEIR SERENE HIGHNESSES PRINCE AND PRINCESS BENTHEIM AND STEINFURT ..	343, 344, 348, Lancaster Tower	Dresser ....158, Lancaster Tower Jager ....159, Lancaster Tower	
HER SERENE HIGHNESS PRINCESS ALIX OF SCHAUMBURG-LIPPE	507 North State Rooms ..	Dresser ....142, North Front	
H.E. COUNTESS ÜXKÜLL GYLLENBAND, DAME DU PALAIS..............	448, West Front	Maid ....437, North Front	
CAROLINA, COUNTESS ÜXKÜLL, DAME D'HONNEUR..............	447, West Front	Maid ....437, North Front	
H.E. GENERAL-ADJUTANT FREIHERR VON BILFINGER..............	433, North Front	Valet ....412, Box Lobby	
H.E. FREIHERR VON REISCHACH, OBER-HOFMEISTER DER KONIGIN	449, West Front..........	Valet ....451, West Front	
FLÜGEL-ADJUTANT MAJOR MOHN	432, North Front	Valet ....457, Box Lobby	
LA BARONNE VAN ITTERSUM, DAME DU PALAIS DE LA REINE, AND DAME D'HONNEUR DE LA REINE MÈRE	178, 179, Edward 3rd's Tower	Maid ....68, Edward 3rd's Tower	
MDLLE. VAN DE POLL, DAME DU PALAIS DE LA REINE, AND DAME D'HONNEUR DE LA REINE MÈRE	178, 179, Edward 3rd's Tower	Maid ....73, Edward 3rd's Tower	
MONSIEUR VAN WEEDE, MARECHAL DE LA COUR DE LA REINE MÈRE	428, North Front	Valet ....436, North Front	
CHEVALIER PAUW VON WIELDRICHT, CHAMBERLAIN DE LA COUR DE LA REINE MÈRE..........	426, North Front	Valet ....436, North Front	

Guests who stayed at Windsor for the marriage of Princess Alice of Albany with Prince Alexander of Teck. Every corner of the castle was packed with visitors. 'The foreigners mostly *very plain*', noted Louisa.

The Queen Mother of the Netherlands.

The Duke of Saxe-Coburg.

Ceremonial

TO BE OBSERVED AT

The Marriage of HER ROYAL HIGHNESS THE PRINCESS ALICE MARY VICTORIA AUGUSTA PAULINE, Daughter of HIS LATE ROYAL HIGHNESS THE DUKE OF ALBANY and of HER ROYAL HIGHNESS THE DUCHESS OF ALBANY, and Niece of THEIR MAJESTIES THE KING AND QUEEN, with HIS SERENE HIGHNESS THE PRINCE ALEXANDER AUGUSTUS FREDERICK WILLIAM ALFRED GEORGE OF TECK, K.C.V.O., D.S.O., in St. George's Chapel, Windsor Castle, on Wednesday, the 10th of February, 1904, at 12.30 o'clock.

Their Majesties' Guests invited to be present at the Ceremony will travel from London by Special Train leaving Paddington Station at 10.45 o'clock, and will proceed at once to the West Entrance to St. George's Chapel, when, together with those at the Castle and resident in the neighbourhood, they will be shewn to seats in the Choir by His Majesty's Gentlemen Ushers.

The ceremonial to be observed at the marriage.

RUSSIA AND JAPAN
FACE TO FACE IN THE FAR EAST.
The Question of the Railway.

"Nothing can be more futile than to declaim against the partition of China and in favour of the integrity of this Asiatic Empire when the soldier of words *is confronted with steel rails* and uniformed guards and the flag of a great Power."— Senator A. J. Beveridge (U.S.A.)

'First shot between Japan and Russia', 7 February 1904. The Court, including Queen Alexandra, the Tsar's aunt, were nearly all on the side of Japan.

The wedding group. 'A most cheerful wedding', wrote Princess May, 'no crying and Aunt Helen [the bride's mother] behaved like a brick.'

WINDSOR CASTLE.

Countess of Antrim

In Corette Tapestry Room
On 10th in St George's Hall

DINNER SITTING LIST. TUESDAY, 9TH FEBRUARY, 1904.

Lieut.-Col Hon. H. C. Legge	Major Wray
Freiherr von Eschen	Capt. Walter Campbell
Lady Collins	Hon. Derek Keppel
Major Mohn	Miss Emily Loch
Hon. Mary Dyke	Hon. John Ward
Freiherr von Hadeln	Lady Knollys
Hon. Mrs. Egerton	Chevalier Pauw von Wveildricht
Sir A. Condie Stephen	Countess of Airlie
Fräulein von Mauve	General Sir Godfrey Clerk
Lord Suffield	Carolina, Countess Uskült
H. E. Countess Uskült	Viscount Churchill
Earl of Erroll	The Princess Louise of Wied
The Duchess of Teck	Duke of Portland
The Prince Francis of Teck	The Princess Victoria Patricia of Connaught
The Princess Margaret of Connaught	H. E. General Adjutant von Bilfinger
The Hereditary Prince of Wied	The Princess Alice of Albany
Princess Louis of Battenberg.	The Prince Alexander of Teck
The Prince of Wales	Princess Louise (Duchess of Fife).
The Queen of Würtemberg	The Duke of Connaught
THE KING	THE QUEEN
The Queen Mother of the Netherlands	The Duke of Saxe-Coburg and Gotha
The Prince Charles of Denmark	The Princess of Wales
The Hereditary Princess of Wied	The Prince Christian of Schleswig-Holstein
The Prince of Waldeck-Pyrmont	The Princess of Waldeck-Pyrmont
The Princess Christian of Schleswig-Holstein	The Prince Arthur of Connaught
The Prince of Bentheim	The Princess of Bentheim
The Princess Victoria	Prince Louis of Battenberg
The Duke of Teck	The Duchess of Albany
The Duchess of Connaught	Duke of Argyll
Duke of Fife	The Princess Victoria of Schleswig-Holstein
The Princess Alexandra of Schaumburg Lippe	Freiherr von Reischach
Earl of Clarendon	The Duchess of Buccleuch
Baronne von Ittersum	Monsieur van Weede
Lord Knollys	Countess of Antrim
Mlle. van de Poll	Flügel Adjutant von Aptel
Colonel Egerton	Miss Heron Maxwell
Hon. Charlotte Knollys	Hauptmann von Gillhausen
Colonel Brockleburst	Miss Nona Kerr
Hon. Sylvia Edwardes	Sir Robert Collins

Seating list for dinner
on the eve of the wedding.

The bride's mother,
the Duchess of Albany.

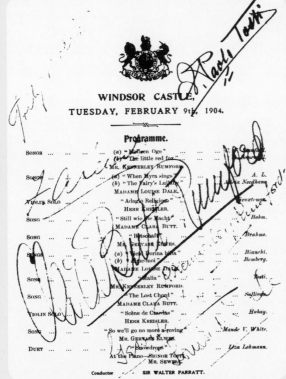

WINDSOR CASTLE,
TUESDAY, FEBRUARY 9th, 1904.

Programme.

SONGS	(a) "Molleen Oge"	
	(b) "The little red fox"	
	MR. KENNERLEY RUMFORD	
SONGS	(a) "When Myra sings"	A. L.
	(b) "The Fairy's Lullaby"	Alicia Needham
	MADAME LOUISE DALE	
VIOLIN SOLO	"Adagio Religioso"	Benztmann
	HERR KREISLER	
SONG	"Still wie die Nacht"	Bohm
	MADAME CLARA BUTT	
SONG	"Botschaft"	Brahms
	MR. GERVASE ELWES	
SONGS	(a) "Sien Dorina bella"	Bianchi
	(b) "Aspemot"	Bemberg
	MADAME LOUISE DALE	
SONG	"Mattinata"	Tosti
	MR. KENNERLEY RUMFORD	
SONG	"The Lost Chord"	Sullivan
	MADAME CLARA BUTT	
VIOLIN SOLO	"Scène de Csardas"	Hubay
	HERR KREISLER	
SONG	"So we'll go no more a-roving"	Maude V. White
	MR. GERVASE ELWES	
DUET	"Snowdrops"	Liza Lehmann

At the Piano — SIGNOR TOSTI
MR. SEWELL

Conductor — SIR WALTER PARRATT.

After-dinner concert in the Waterloo Gallery.
Louisa had supper with the artistes afterwards.

St. George's Hall, where 100 guests
dined after the wedding.

Waterford.
Dudley.

The Viceregal Lodge, Dublin.

The new royal yacht _Victoria & Albert_, which had been built at enormous cost in 1901.

The Countess of Dudley, a famous society beauty.

The Earl of Dudley, the Lord Lieutenant of Ireland. He provided lavish hospitality largely at his own expense.

TIME TABLE

AND

SYNOPSIS OF PROGRAMME

OF

THEIR MAJESTIES
VISIT TO IRELAND.

APRIL, 1904.

ULSTER'S OFFICE,
DUBLIN CASTLE.

State visit to Ireland.
Louisa accompanied the King and Queen.

Houseparty at the Viceregal Lodge. Louisa, second from the left, stands with Charlotte Knollys and Lady Londonderry.

1904.

County and City of Kilkenny Agricultural Society.

PROGRAMME

...OF THE...

Horse Jumping

Competitions.

—Commencing at 2.30 p.m. To-Day.—

—SATURDAY, 30th APRIL, 1904.—

Jumping Enclosure,

ST. JAMES'S PARK, KILKENNY.

M. M. MURPHY, Hon. Secretary,
Parliament-St., Kilkenny.

Price - - - 3d.

"Journal" Office]

Programme for the Horse Show at Kilkenny.
It was followed by fireworks and a party
at Kilkenny Castle.

Racing at Leopardstown, 'the prettiest meeting imaginable'.
It was the kind of function the King also much enjoyed.

Two days later, the royal procession arrives
for the races at Phoenix Park.

Kilkenny Castle, a splendid medieval castle
above the river Suir.

Lady Ormonde, with whom
the royal party stayed
at Kilkenny Castle.

VISIT OF

THEIR MAJESTIES

KING EDWARD VII.

AND

QUEEN ALEXANDRA.

—

LUNCHEON

IN THE COUNCIL CHAMBER,

2nd May, 1904.

CITY HALL,
WATERFORD.

Luncheon with the Mayor at Waterford,
with the processions before and after.

Group in the Long Gallery, Kilkenny Castle. Louisa stands second from the left.

The King presenting an address at Waterford.

Lismore Castle.   Co. Waterford

Lismore Castle on the river Blackwater, the Duke of Devonshire's house in Ireland, and the last staging-post of the royal visit.

The Duchess of Devonshire.

The Duke of Devonshire.

The King planting a tree at Lismore.

An optimistic 'loyal' farewell anthem for the King and Queen
at Kingstown Harbour, Dublin.

River Blackwater at Lismore.   Co. Waterford

View from Louisa's window at Lismore:
the river Blackwater.

THIS CARD WILL NOT ADMIT.

Visit to the City of
Their Majesties the King & Queen of Portugal.

The Corporation of London requests the honor of the Company of

The Countess of Antrim

at a Dejeiiner in the Guildhall on Thursday the 17th of November 1904.
at Half-past Twelve o'clock P.M.

The favor of an immediate answer addressed to The Town Clerk Guildhall EC is requested.
and if the Invitation be accepted, a Card of Admission with particulars will be forwarded.

LEVÉE DRESS, UNIFORM OR EVENING DRESS.

The state visit of the King and Queen of Portugal:
Louisa's invitation to a luncheon at the Guildhall.

Visit of Their Majesties
The King and Queen
of Portugal
to the City of London.

17th November, 1904.

Menu for the luncheon, which
was well up to the King
of Portugal's famous appetite
(there were meringues 'Maids of
Honour' for pudding).

Guests at Windsor to meet the
Portuguese King and Queen.
Above: Lord Curzon, Viceroy of
India; below: Lord Salisbury
(who had succeeded his father
in 1903), Lord Privy Seal.

Queen Amélie of Portugal. She embarrassed King Edward by
giving him smacking kisses, but Louisa found her 'charming'.

Shooting party near Virginia Water. The ladies joined the shooters for luncheon;
Louisa is standing, second from the left.

"MONSIEUR BEAUCAIRE"

A Romantic Comedy in Four Acts

By BOOTH TARKINGTON and E. G. SUTHERLAND

Monsieur Beaucaire	-	Mr. LEWIS WALLER
Duke of Winterset	-	Mr. EDWARD FERRIS
Major Molyneux	-	Mr. FRANK DYALL
Lord Townbrake	-	Mr. CHARLES GOODHALT
Mr. Bantison	-	Mr. W. GAYER MACKAY
Mr. Rakell	-	Mr. NORMAN McKINNEL
Mr. Bicksett	-	Mr. A. E. GEORGE
Beau Nash	-	Mr. CHARLES ALLAN
Captain Badger	-	Mr. S. B. BRERETON
Marquis de Mirepoix	-	Mr. ARTHUR LEWIS
Francois	-	Mr. H. SAVILE
Jolliffe	-	Mr. J. BYRON
Servant	-	Mr. C. McGUINNESS
Lady Mary Carlyle	-	Miss EVELYN MILLARD
Lucy Rellerton	-	Miss CONSTANCE WALTON
Mrs. Mabsley	-	Miss KATE TYNDALL
Lady Rellerton	-	Miss MAY CHENERY
Miss Presbury	-	Miss CATHERINE VYSE
Miss Paitelot	-	Miss MARY LEWIS
Countess of Greenbury	-	Miss MINNIE GRIFFIN

Guests, Servants, etc. :
Misses WINIFRED GODARD, MAUD VYSE, ELEANOR MAY,
MAUD DIGAN.
Messrs. JOHN BEAUCHAMP, HENRY J. CARVILL,
OWEN ROUGHWOOD, ERIC SCOTT FRANK WOOLFE,
PATRICK DIGAN, A. GABRIEL, C. LE BUTT.

The action of the Play takes place at Bath.
Period - 1735.

ACT I. - - - - The Pump Room
(One Week elapses)

ACT II. Scene 1. - - Beaucaire's Lodgings
Scene 2. - Ballroom at Lady Rellerton's
(Two Weeks elapse)

ACT III. - - - The Park at Mr. Bantison's
(One Week elapses)

ACT IV. - - - The Pump Room

General Manager - Mr. LYSTON LYLE
Stage Manager - Mr. W. W. KEENE

'Monsieur Beaucaire', a farce acted for the Court's amusement after dinner one evening at Windsor.

The Tapestry Room, where the concert was held. It had been splendidly redecorated since Queen Victoria's death.

WINDSOR CASTLE.

NOVEMBER 18th, 1904.

—o—

PROGRAMME.

1.	(a) "When the swallows homeward fly"	M. V. White
	(b) "Rose of Killarney"	C. Villiers Stanford
	MR. KENNERLY RUMFORD	
2.	ROMANZA (Mignon)	Ambroise Thomas
	MELLE. RINA GIACHETTI	
3.	ROMANZA (Luisa Miller)	Verdi
	SIGNOR ANSELMI	
4.	(a) "My heart is weary"	Goring Thomas
	(b) "Si mes vers avaient des ailes"	R. Hahn
	MADAME CLARA BUTT	
5.	DUET (La Bohème)	Puccini
	MELLE. RINA GIACHETTI and SIGNOR ANSELMI	
6.	"Off to Philadelphia"	Battison Haynes
	MR. KENNERLY RUMFORD	
7.	"Mia Piccirella" (Salvator Rosa)	Gomez
	MELLE. RINA GIACHETTI	
8.	(a) "Vorrei"	Tosti
	(b) "Aprile"	Tosti
	SIGNOR ANSELMI.	
	Accompanied by the Composer.	
9.	"The Lost Chord"	Sullivan
	MADAME CLARA BUTT	
10.	QUARTETT (Rigoletto)	Verdi
	MELLE. GIACHETTI, MME. BUTT, SIGNOR ANSELMI, and MR. RUMFORD.	

Accompanist—MR. S. LIDDLE.

Conductor—SIR WALTER PARRATT.

Concert in the Tapestry Room, 18 November.

MR. LEWIS WALLER
AS "MONSIEUR BEAUCAIRE," IN WHICH PART HE APPEARS
AT WINDSOR CASTLE LAST SATURDAY.

Mr Lewis Waller
as 'Monsieur Beaucaire'.

To Lady Antrim

WITH right hearty GREETINGS for a HAPPY CHRISTMAS.

Brief words say much, and dark and drear December Turns smiling June when absent friends remember!
Clifton Bingham.

FROM Amélie

Though distance divides Yet FRIENDSHIP abides.

Christmas card to Louisa from Queen Amélie, December 1904.

MEDITERRANEAN SPRING

BY ROYAL YACHT TO SICILY, ITALY, CORFU, GREECE AND PORTUGAL. THE SPANISH MARRIAGE. 1905-1906

For some reason, Louisa's picture album of 1905 has been lost. But her diary for this date shows that her Princess of the year would have been the much underestimated Princess Victoria ('Toria') of Wales. Poor Toria was the home-bound sister of the three. At her mother's beck and call, she had a long nose and also tended to pull a long face (in Edwardian idiom), from general frustration. Louisa was her natural comforter, and she Louisa's most faithful royal correspondent. When Sybil had another baby in 1905 and Lady Minto became Vicereine of India, it was Victoria who wrote to congratulate. Their friendship seems to have blossomed during a yacht trip this year, when the Princess conveyed her sorrows – love? mother trouble? sibling trouble? – to Louisa. '*Victoria & Albert* [undated]. Bless you! for what you wrote. Oh! so lovely just what I WANTED. . . . I shall treasure it all my life & of course keep it *quite private*. . . . I am a fool I know but somehow you seemed to understand so much without words. . . . Goodnight! – V.' She confided to Louisa on 28 August, 'I have again passed through *black* days & I try to remember our nice talks on board! & it helps one on'. Louisa also was 'sad at writing Finis to such a happy time'. Fortunately it was not Finis. For the trip was to be repeated in 1906.

The political situation, however, had changed. There had been a crushing Tory electoral defeat that winter. The Kaiser rather hoped that the Liberal victory would mean an end to Britain's Entente Cordiale with France, signed in 1904, and a rapprochement with Germany. However, the new Liberal Foreign Minister, Sir Edward Grey, accepted the Entente and a bi-partisan foreign policy. Indeed Germany's sabre-rattling at Algeciras in Morocco was rapidly turning the Anglo-French agreement into a military alliance. In the words of Gordon Brook–Shepherd (*Uncle of Europe*, 1975), 'the Entente Cordiale was already changing out of its frock coat and into uniform'.

King Edward's avuncular European trips usually combined business with pleasure. This time he intended to investigate some little local difficulties in Greece, after which he would look in on Italy and pay a visit to England's oldest ally, Portugal. Leaving Alice Keppel behind at Biarritz, now his preferred French resort (he too, like Lord Salisbury, found a plethora of royalties and flies in Cannes and Nice), he joined his wife at Marseilles on the *Victoria & Albert*, commanded by another of the 'favorita' family, Captain Colin Keppel. The handsome Commodore of the royal yacht was a great admirer of Louisa, once writing to her, 'You were always our own "particular" Lady'.

They reached Messina on 9 April, going straight on 'by Special' to 'quaint little' Taormina, where they saw Etna 'kindly unveiled for our benefit'. Corfu was both 'glorious' and imposing, because of the Palace (once the lonely Empress of Austria's Achilleon), the Villa Mon Repos and the panorama of ships and admirals, the Greek King having joined their Majesties on board and the Prince and Princess of Wales arriving back from their Indian tour on the *Renown*. Louisa was to see two volcanoes, Etna and Vesuvius, on this trip. There was always the risk of a third – King Edward. The sight of any deviation from the precisely correct uniform would provoke an explosion. Admiral Lord Charles Beresford's present failure to receive King George of the Hellenes in full dress uniform was later to prejudice the King in favour of Admiral 'Jackie' Fisher, Beresford's opponent on naval strategy. On this occasion it was surprisingly not the admirals that Louisa picked out for their charms, but the torpedo practice – 'delightful' – and the target practice – 'very pretty'.

To Louisa, the visit to Athens, where they arrived on 17 April, unluckily centred on the Olympic Games, revived a decade ago after a lapse of just over sixteen hundred years. If the Games had remained in abeyance for another century Louisa would have felt no regret. 'About ¼ to 3 we went to the Stadium, when the Games began – they were tedious the sun was hot & we sat almost 4 mortal hours. We all nearly died of it.' That evening she looked at the floodlit Acropolis 'peacefully' from her sitting-room. Meanwhile the King was doing his state business quietly behind the scenes. Within two months the unpopular Prince George of Crete had been withdrawn from his governorship of the island. After the *Victoria & Albert* had sailed for Naples, Louisa received an amusing letter and pictures from Prince Nicholas of Greece, with whom she had lunched. Prince Nicholas felt 'quite queer' after the visitors had left, 'as Athens very quickly went back to its old appearance of supreme quietness and monotony'. The local babies had been overfed by the British sailors on tea and cakes, '& I daresay felt very emancipated'.

The expedition to Vesuvius was sadly lacking in cakes or anything else to eat. Louisa was to confide years afterwards to her grandchildren that when they reached the summit they found the picnic basket had been left behind. 'I am a humble man, a simple man', Louisa wailed, mimicking the anguished King, 'all I ask is a *sandwich*.' There was a further scene at Naples when Lord Rosebery, who had entertained them the day before in his beautiful Villa Posillipo, arrived for dinner on the royal yacht in a mess jacket *and white tie*. This solecism ruined the King's evening. And perhaps Princess Victoria's also? For a time she seems to have hoped to marry the widowed Rosebery. No doubt she had felt human envy on hearing that her much younger first cousin, Princess Ena of Battenberg, was engaged to King Alfonso XIII of Spain. The Kaiser saw this match as part of the plot to 'encircle' Germany: 'The whole of these pathetic and degenerate Latins', he lamented, 'are becoming tools in England's hands.'

King Alfonso and Princess Ena were married in Madrid Cathedral at the end of May. The ceremony was 'perfect', but as they left the Cathedral for the wedding breakfast at the Palace, an anarchist threw a bomb at their state coach. The enraged crowd closed in on him. Seeing that he had succeeded in killing and maiming only innocent bystanders, coachmen and horses, he killed himself. Louisa received the news – 'so cruel & horrible' – at Glenarm; there followed a letter from Princess Beatrice, Queen Ena's mother. Though 'poor dear Ena' had been exposed to such a 'diabolical act', she was now recovered from the shock '& looking fresh & well, & beamingly happy'.

Louisa's diary for 1906 also ended on a happier note, with a list of the presents she had bought on the cruise. For the Queen, 'tray & Bird', for Princess Victoria, 'silver figure', for Charlotte Knollys, 'Venetian glass & bottle', for Sir Charles Hardinge, 'frame'. . . . Royal Presents received were: Easter eggs from the King, Queen and Princess Victoria; a gold owl from the King; a Medusa head, marble Madonna, Venetian chain and china lampstand from the Queen; a picture, Venetian glass and 'worked bag' from Princess Victoria.

Royal Special Train, Victoria to Dover Pier, travelling via Chatham and Canterbury.

The S.E. & C. Railway Co.'s Turbine Steamer "Invicta" will perform the Channel crossing to Calais.

Lunch will be served at Calais, and the journey will thence be made in a Royal Special composed of Royal Saloons Nos. 1 and 3 and one "Aldy." Carriage of the Northern of France Railway.

A Restaurant Car will be attached to the Train at the Gare de Lyon, Paris, where Dinner will be served after departure at 7.40 p.m.

The Restaurant Car will be run through from Paris to Marseilles.

French Railway Time is five minutes in advance of Greenwich Time.

Journey to MARSEILLES
OF
HER MAJESTY QUEEN ALEXANDRA
AND SUITE.

Monday, April 2nd, 1906.

VICTORIA	dep.	11 30 a.m.
Dover Pier	{ arr.	1 20 p.m.
	{ dep.	1 30 „
Calais Maritime	{ arr.	2 45 „
(French Time)	{ dep.	3 30 „
Paris (Gare de Lyon)	{ arr.	7 23 „
	{ dep.	7 40 „
Dijon	{ arr.	11 50 „
	{ dep.	11 56 „
Lyons	{ arr.	2 27 a.m.
	{ dep.	2 33 „
Avignon	{ arr.	5 25 „
	{ dep.	5 33 „
Estaque	{ arr.	6 57 „
	{ dep.	6 58 „
MARSEILLES PORT, Mole C	arr.	7 30 „

The 'Special' to Marseilles to meet the royal yacht. Louisa set off on a five-week cruise on 17 April, her second trip with the King and Queen.

Captain Colin Keppel, the handsome Commodore of the royal yacht. He was a great fan of Louisa.

The Greek theatre at Taormina, above Messina.

The royal party visiting the ruins of the Greek theatre.

The dining-saloon on board the royal yacht *Victoria & Albert*.

Preparing to receive the King of Greece on board the royal yacht. King Edward was a stickler for correct dress.

View of the citadel at Corfu.

Dinner to the
Prince & Princess of Wales
Ap: 11. 190   *& the King of Greece*

Crème d'Epinards

Truites à la Bordelaise

Côtelettes de Volaille, Pajarsky

Aloyau rôti

Cailles à la Broche

Asperges de Laurio Sce Mousseuse

Charlotte à la Reine

Compôte de Pêches

Croûtes au Jambon

Glace à l'orange

Corfou   11 Avril 1906

Dinner on the *Victoria & Albert* for the King of Greece
and the Prince and Princess of Wales,
who were on their way back from India.

The British fleet outside Corfu – a magnificent scene.

Princess May.

Mon Repos, the King of Greece's villa on Corfu.

Louisa with Lady Shaftesbury ('Cuckoo'),
Princess May's Lady in Waiting.

Dîner du 12 Avril 1906.

Corfu

Tortue Clair

Filets de Merlans Chevreuse

Mousse de Jambon Clamart

Cailles à la Richelieu

Selles d'Agneau

Chapons rôtis

Asperges Sce Blanche

Chartreuse de Pêches

Soufflé glacé Tosca

Flan Suisse

Coupes Jacques

Dinner on board H.M.S. *Renown*,
the Prince of Wales's yacht.

The King of Greece's luncheon party
at Mon Repos on 12 April.

Corfu – a panoramic view.

To have the 🏴 honour of meeting
Their Majesties The King & Queen
Admiral Lord Charles Beresford
requests the pleasure of
The Countess of Antrim's
Company at Dinner
on Saturday April 14th at 8.30 o'clock.

H.M.S. Bulwark.
Boat at   o'clock
at

By Signal
An answer is requested
to the Flag Lieutenant.

Lord Charles Beresford,
Admiral of the British
Mediterranean fleet.

H.M.S. *Bulwark* off Corfu.

🏴 H.M.S. BULWARK.
MEDITERRANEAN.

FORWARD.

Secretary J. Keys.

PORT SIDE.	STARBOARD SIDE.
Captain M. Culme Seymour	Captain Hon. H. L. Hood
Captain Sheppard	Engineer-Captain Little
Mr. Frank Dugdale	Captain Bacon
Colonel Thompson	Sir Charles Cust
Major F. Ponsonby	Captain Patey
Commodore Colin Keppell	Captain The Hon. S. Fortescue
Mrs. Harrison.	The Rt. Hon. A. Fellows
Lord Cecil Manners	The Hon. Charlotte Knollys
Lady Antrim	Lord Shaftesbury
His Grace The Duke of Leeds	H.R.H. Princess Victoria
Her Majesty The Queen.	H.R.H. The Prince of Wales
Admiral Lord Charles Beresford	Captain Sturdee
His Majesty The King.	H.R.H. The Princess of Wales
Lady Shaftesbury	Lord Howe
Sir Charles Hardinge	Lady Montgomery
Lady Eva Dugdale	Lord Albert Osborne
The Right Hon. Sir H. Maxwel.	Mrs. Mundy
Miss Mundy	Sir Arthur Bigge
Commodore Hon. H. Tyrwhitt	Mr. Mundy
The Hon. H. Stonor	Captain Simons
Captain Sir George Warrender	The Hon. Derek Keppel
Colonel Frederick	Captain Tupper
Captain Brock	Captain Campbell
Commander Sueter	Commander Bruen

[DOOR]

Flag-Lieutenant Gibbs.

AFT.

Seating plan for the dinner on board the
Admiral's battleship, H.M.S. *Bulwark*.

King George of Greece,
Queen Alexandra's brother.

Visit to Athens. Louisa had a fine view
of the Acropolis from her sitting-room.

Queen Olga of Greece, sister of Alexander II of Russia.
She was a brilliant linguist.

Crown Princess Sophie.

Prince George of Crete. His
failure in governing the island
was one of the main reasons
for King Edward's visit.

Crown Prince Constantine
of Greece.

The Kings and Queens entering the stadium for the
Olympic Games, which had been newly revived by King George.

The Games were 'tedious', wrote Louisa. 'The sun was hot & we sat almost 4 mortal hours. We all nearly died of it.'

Expedition to Tatoi. 'Luncheon & tea under the trees.'

The Danish lady gymnasts go through their drill.

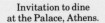

Invitation to dine at the Palace, Athens.

Lawn tennis at Athens. Hats were still obligatory.

The King and Queen landing at Naples.

Expedition to the observatory at Vesuvius, 30 April.

Louisa's sketch of the yacht, with Vesuvius in the background.

Vesuvius erupting. 'Impossible to imagine or describe
the horror of the devastation', noted Louisa.

Destruction caused by the eruption at Torre del Greco
which Louisa visited after the event.

The party had luncheon on
29 April with Lord Rosebery at
his villa at Posillipo. He greatly
annoyed the King the next
day by arriving incorrectly
dressed for dinner.

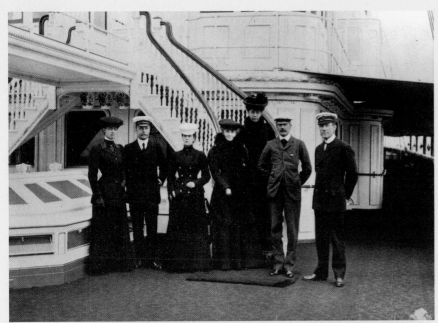

Group on board the *Victoria & Albert*. The Queen, Louisa and Charlotte Knollys stand at the centre, with Princess Victoria to the left and Captain Keppel to the right.

O. S. P. 7 Pisa – Il Campanile.

Expedition to Pisa 6th May 1906

A stop at Pisa
on the return journey.

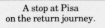

Princess Victoria
sightseeing in Pisa.

Rome – the Tiber, with the Castel S. Angelo in the background;
the Arco di Settimio Severo; the Forum.

Gibraltar from the royal yacht.

Luncheon and tea at Algeciras, 15 May.

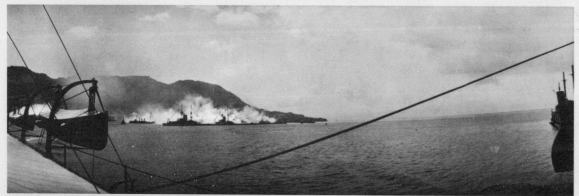

The British fleet saluting the yacht on leaving Gibraltar, 17 May.

Algeciras – a donkey ride to see a waterfall.

The King and Queen of Portugal
with Queen Alexandra.

Real Paço da Pena

ALMOÇO DO DIA 18 DE MAIO DE 1906

MENU

Omelette aux fines herbes

Croquettes

Poulets à l'Allemande

Filet de Bœuf Marivaux

Dindonneau Roti

Terrine de Foie Gras

Asperges sauce Hollandaise

Gateau aux amandes

Luncheon with the Portuguese royal family at Cintra, 18 May.
The drive back to Lisbon was 'at a most alarming pace'.

Tea with friends on 16 May.

A farewell group picture
taken at the end of the cruise.

Engagement photograph of Princess Ena of Battenberg and King
Alfonso of Spain, Spring 1906. 'The young people are absolutely
devoted to each other', wrote Princess Beatrice to Louisa.

Mateo Morral, who threw a bomb at the bridal coach. He killed
himself after the attempt, much to Louisa's approval.

The royal wedding procession through Madrid, just before the bomb attack,
which killed several people and spattered the young King and Queen with blood.

IRISH SUMMER

GARDENING, GRANDCHILDREN
AND MOTOR CARS
AT GLENARM.
1906

Ireland saw a good deal of Louisa during 1906, perhaps because of the welcome Bill gave her on her return from the Mediterranean in May. 'Stormy but warm. Bill very glad to get me home', she wrote. Louisa had also begun the year with an Irish houseparty, at Mountstewart, one of the few places where Bill consented to stay. The Antrims went there every year and the parties were generally glittering with society beauties and men of consequence. The house contained the table on which the famous Lord Castlereagh (later Londonderry) had signed at the Congress of Vienna in 1815. Unfortunately the Lord Castlereagh of 1906 was canvassing his English constituency, and Lady Londonderry with him. Without the dynamic Nellie Londonderry, wrote Louisa, they were 'rather a depressed little party'. On the third day, 'Bill went back to Glenarm early'. Nothing loath, Louisa removed to Killarney, the entrancing home of Lady Kenmare.

But alas, 'appalling' election results began pouring in, like the floods that swept the lakeside. Louisa and Elizabeth Kenmare lunched in 'a pretty little thatched & panelled cottage' by a waterfall feeding the top lake, talking in subdued tones. 'Elections sickening – hardly a Unionist left. . . .' At least Killarney, even in sleet and snow, was 'a revelation . . . & must be a paradise in summer'.

In summer, life at Glenarm was enhanced by the grandchildren, for the exquisite Sybil managed to keep up her singing to a professional standard as well as having a baby every other year. The only tragedy was that poor Ducie and his wife Margaret (Peg) Talbot had had 'a beautiful boy' in 1905 and another in 1907, both weighing over nine pounds and both born dead. (They were later to have a family.) At his son's wedding the Buzzard had been particularly farouche. 'How lucky Peg is to be marrying Dunluce', said one of the Talbots pleasantly; 'he has such a head on his shoulders.' 'So has a pin', replied the Buzzard. (Jock Balfour, Ducie's cousin, defends him as 'a golden-hearted and extremely shrewd little man'.)

Louisa had a familiar round of duties and pleasures: letters, accounts, 'arranging' (like her Sovereign), visiting the village school and sewing class, and bicycling up to the farm and back, 'shockingly out of condition' when she tried it that July. But her growing interest was in her garden. This year she invited the famous amateur gardener, Miss Willmott, author of *Genus Rosa*, to advise her on her Frau Karl Drushki roses. Louisa wrote: 'dragged Bill to the garden – he was delighted with the roses.' Miss Willmott photographed some of the beds for Louisa, while Louisa painted the herbaceous border in water-colours. But Louisa's favourite retreat and private kingdom was the wild garden surrounding her summerhouse. Here she wrestled with bulbs in the long grass. Her labours completed, she would repose on a *chaise longue*, attended by singing birds in cages.

Times were changing even at Glenarm, with its medieval air carefully fostered by the battlements and Barbican Gate. Visitors were becoming more frequent, much to Louisa's delight, and not only because of the bicycle but also because of the motor car. Strangers on bicycles could of course still cause the Buzzard annoyance. One day a hotgospeller arrived at Glenarm on a bicycle. 'Are you saved, my lord?' he asked with evangelical fervour. 'Certainly.' 'Are you quite sure, my lord?' 'Cock.' 'My lord, I see you dislike religion.' 'It isn't religion I dislike but your filthy fingernails.'

The fingernails of motorists were often equally filthy, since their vehicles were always breaking down. Nevertheless the motors kept appearing at Glenarm. On 6 August there were three motors at the door at the same time. This 'uncommon event' overwhelmed Louisa. 'I felt quite weak.' The age of motoring had in fact arrived. The King had his claret-coloured Daimlers and Mercedes; the Queen had her wild enthusiasm for fast driving. 'I did enjoy being driven about . . . at fifty miles an hour!' she wrote. 'I poke [our driver] in the back at every corner to go gently. . . .' Foreign royalties tended to terrorize their passengers. Fritz Ponsonby described a hair-raising drive with the brother of the King of Portugal.

Louisa's first experience of motoring at Glenarm was in 1901, when 'Mr Morgan [Jack] took me and Mabel in his motor – wh: was the most heavenly thing I ever did . . . the rain beginning as we returned – drenching us to the skin'. The Morgans returned next year. This time, despite 'appalling' roads, they covered fifty miles in just under four delirious hours. By 1903 the Buzzard was a motorist. 'Bill took Sybil & me on the car', wrote Louisa, '& we drove up the park – tho' it shook & jolted horribly.' It was a scarlet steam car, known to his family as 'the Fire-Engine'. But his car was not to make him any less anti-social. Suffering from gout, he was leaving a houseparty at Newton Don, his sister Nina Balfour's home, before the other guests were awake. The party was in honour of Princess Thora, known as 'the Snipe' because of her very long nose. The Buzzard, as he departed, hooted unmercifully under the Snipe's windows, saying to his young nephew Jock, 'A good thing for her to be treated in this way'. Ducie and Peg drove away from their wedding of 1904 in a car, and that August Jessie Morgan prepared for a motoring holiday at Glenarm. Louisa began as usual in ecstasies: 'delightful motor . . . quite heavenly it was – & made distance of no account' – until, horrors, 'unfortunately a spring broke so it had to go & mend'.

This year, 1906, Louisa boldly hired herself a car for the regular Larne–Glenarm journey. She was feeling rather the worse for wear, having suffered during her waiting at Windsor from an inflamed leg and one 'terribly long stand' after another. Even Queen Alexandra could be ruthless about standing. There was a story of the Queen overhearing a Lord in Waiting murmur, 'Are we never to sit down tonight?' Promptly Alexandra dragged up a chair – 'Poor thing, he is so tired' – and sat him down in it until the King's arrival put a term to his humiliation.

Louisa now added a new list in her diary to those she already made of books read, presents given and received, days spent in waiting and at Glenarm – a record of her motoring. 'Aug. 12. Motor from Larne 12 miles. . . . 13th. Motor not used. . . . 14th. Motor Larne 24 Miles. . . . 15th. Motor broke down. . . . 22nd. Motor repairing. . . . 23rd. Motor not used.' On the 25th the motor actually did forty-two miles. But Louisa's great moment was to come two years later. 'We heard from Mr Jack [Morgan] that he has bought a Renault for me – wh: is a real pleasure . . . a beauty' – until, horrors again, 'we were punctured'. Back to 'a hireling'. But next year 'Brassington the temporary chauffeur arrived' and the summer motoring record was up to 2587 miles in 114 days; '22 miles daily!'

The Barbican gate at Glenarm.

Family group at Glenarm.

Sybil's children at Glenarm.

Sybil and Rufus.

Glenarm river. Yachting friends could drop anchor just below the castle.

Mr and Mrs Guy Dawnay,
visitors at Glenarm.

The garden photographed by Miss Willmott, the famous gardening expert.

A glimpse of the castle from the lawn, Glenarm.

Louisa and the Buzzard in the hayfield – he farmed his estate
in person, unlike most Irish landlords of the period.

Sybil in picture hat.

The drawing-room, Glenarm,
after Louisa's 'arrangements'.

The Buzzard's red steamcar, known as 'the Fire-Engine'. He had a special rod
with which to open gates, so that he could drive round his estate without getting out.

The view from Louisa's window, with Scottish mountains just visible.

The Buzzard with Ducie's daughter Rose.

Photograph by Miss Willmott. She came in 1905 to give Louisa gardening advice.

A sketch by Louisa of the village, looking towards the sea.

The garden hut, Louisa's favourite retreat.
She planted a 'wilderness' garden around it, of bulbs and shrub roses.

Sybil's children Mary and Stephen.

The Buzzard setting out for a tour of the estate.

The Barbican tower and bridge.

Sybil's fourth child, Stephen.

Bright irises bordering a garden path:
another photograph by Miss Willmott.

Louisa's son Angus
and friends at Walney.

An afternoon on the beach; Rufus paddles.

Granddaughter Mary off to dig in the sand – by Louisa.

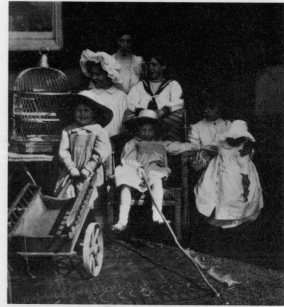

Five grandchildren.

Vere, Mary and Stephen by the sea.

View from the shore at Glenarm,
painted by Louisa.

View across the bay from Glenarm
to the Scottish coast, twenty-five miles away.

IRISH MANSION TURNED INTO AN HOTEL.

On the wild seacoast of Antrim, eighteen miles from the town of Larne, is a beautiful castellated residence, known as Garron Tower. It was built in 1848, by Frances Anne Marchioness of Londonderry, and granddaughter of the last Marquis of Antrim, "in the hope, with the permission of Providence, to establish a residence in her portion of the ancestral domains, and to live in the affections of a devoted and loyal tenantry." No trouble nor expense were spared to beautify the grounds, and to decorate the interior of the house, which is built on a gigantic landslip on the side of a cliff looking out on the Atlantic.

Rows of cannon are placed along the terrace walk, the hall is hung with regimental flags and banners, and all the doors are elaborately carved with figures. The ball-room has a parqueted floor, and wainscoted walls, brightened by coloured armorial bearings. This beautiful house was left by Lady Londonderry to her grandson, Lord Herbert Vane-Tempest. He found it so expensive to keep up, that he recently let it on a twenty-one years' lease to a gentleman, who has converted it into an hotel. The guests are therefore able to revel in genuine ancestral halls.

The fate of a neighbouring castle on the Antrim coast.

Mr and Mrs Jack Pierpont Morgan.

Mrs Jack Pierpont Morgan and Louisa. The Morgans visited every year by yacht.

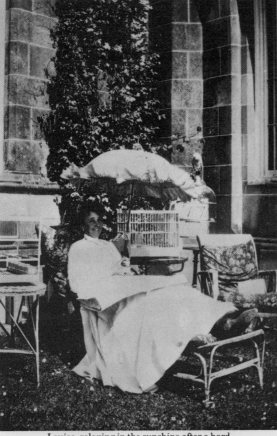

Louisa, relaxing in the sunshine after a hard morning's gardening, with her pet birds beside her.

Louisa's first motor car, complete with chauffeur. She was a passionate enthusiast, despite endless punctures.

ROYAL DIPLOMACY

SPAIN, ITALY AND GREECE.
FRIENDS AT CLIVEDEN.
1907

On 4 April, Louisa wrote 'Busy stopping a cold, wh: made me feel extremely cheap'. Cheap was the wrong word for what lay ahead. In two days Louisa was to start on her third, most lavish Mediterranean cruise with Queen Alexandra; a cruise when they would virtually meet a King in every port, and Edward VII would scoop one of the Kings firmly into the allied net.

Cartagena, on the south-east coast of Spain, was to be the first scene of this 'Yacht Diplomacy', King Alfonso XIII the catch. Queen Alexandra's party joined King Edward's at Toulon. They spent a rough first night at sea, the *Victoria & Albert* 'plunging into that evil Gulf of Lyons', as Louisa put it. After which there was nothing evil to fear – except typhoid in Cartagena. Even this epidemic, however, was a blessing in disguise. For it meant their Majesties could not land. In any case King Edward had no intention of risking the assassin's bullet. His niece Queen Ena of Spain had had her white satin wedding-gown spattered with blood. Her uncle was determined to keep himself unspotted, from his toes to the white top of his yachting cap.

While Louisa was dashing off her diary impressions of 'deafening' salutes from 'an avenue of iron-clads', a 'big luncheon' and 'huge dinner on the *Victoria & Albert* for the Spaniards, and a return visit to Alfonso's yacht *Giralda*, King Edward was negotiating his pact. It was signed on 8 April; another blow to the Kaiser who had not quite given up hope of a cooperative Spain, if Germany ever fought France. Nothing of this seeped into Louisa's diary. On the crucial day, her one anxiety was lest she and her colleagues should fail to sign the Queen Mother's visitors' book on board the *Giralda*. 'After tea', wrote Louisa, 'I went with Lord Howe & Sidney Greville to try to find the Queen's book to write names in – but returned foiled.' Greville was Groom in Waiting to King Edward and Lord Howe was Queen Alexandra's Chamberlain. Years ago Lord Howe's ancestor had been Chamberlain to Queen Adelaide. '*Lord how* wonderful are thy works!' declared a scurrilous broadsheet, circulating the lie that he had got the childless Queen with child. Alexandra had her devotees but was never defamed. As for Queen Maria Christina's book, no doubt it was buried under the mass of treasures Alfonso had brought from the Palace at Madrid to furnish his floating palace.

They left Cartagena on the tenth for renewed 'Yacht Diplomacy', this time at Gaeta in Italy. On their way they stopped at Malta, where the King's nephew by marriage, Prince Louis of Battenberg, was Vice-Admiral of the Mediterranean Fleet, and where Admiral 'Jackie' Fisher entertained them on *Enchantress*. These two men were to be leading figures in the first year of a war that Edward the Peacemaker was still working to prevent.

Gaeta was the site for an Anglo-Italian royal encounter even more painful to the Kaiser than Cartagena. For Italy was at least nominally in the German camp. Nevertheless their Britannic Majesties and suites were feasted on board the *Trincatria*, King Victor Emmanuel's yacht. They were glad to have '*rosbif à l'anglais*' on the menu, for the weather was suddenly 'chilly'. But not so chilly as the German-speaking press. Though the Gaeta handshake was intended by the two Kings merely to signify friendship all round, a Viennese paper called it the attempt to *einzukreisen* (encircle) Germany.

Meanwhile the royal yacht entered yet other ports, the Italian Ambassador in London dining on board her in Naples. There was 'glorious sunshine – wh: warmed the heart' and brought out the cameras. Plenty for Louisa to photograph: famous gardens and churches, their Majesties, and friends like Charlotte Knollys and Fritz Ponsonby. Appropriately, the opera in Naples was called *L'Amico Fritz*, and a royal villa they visited in Palermo had the familiar name of 'La Favorita'. How the Lords and Ladies in Waiting must have giggled, though of course Mrs Keppel was not present. On 26 April came 'the exit from Palermo in a beautiful sunset, quite lovely', followed by the return to Naples, for poor Louisa to have 'a nasty feverish chill'. Within two days she was again shopping and dining: 'bought a few odds & ends & tho' a little tired not too much so. The Captains from the Cruisers etc. dined, & we played Bridge.'

Corfu again. Louisa confessed she had hardly realized last year how glorious it was, especially the views from the gun batteries. All seemed set for perpetual lotus-eating. 'May 6. At Sea. The most perfect yachting day I ever knew – hot enough to sit under the awning without a jacket – & here I read & wrote all day – passing between the Greek Islands. Threading through Ithaca & Cephalonia wonderfully beautiful.' Louisa does not seem to have read about Ulysses and his faithful Penelope as they sighted Ithaca. Perhaps she was too much unlike Penelope – no stay-at-home she. Instead she perused *The Open Road* and *Wages of Sin*, with possibly a dutiful glance at *Architecture for the General Reader* and *Fabian Essays*. Alas, they were soon in port again. 'May 7. Grilling heat – we arrived at the Piraeus at 11.30.' Luncheon for the Greek royalties on board. 'At 3 we moved on to the Palace – & we sadly settled in.'

The word 'grilling' dominated Louisa's Athens diary, and the Stadium events were again 'rather wearying', a Palace banquet 'rather tiresome'. There were none the less 'most beautiful' moments in the country – at Marathon with Prince and Princess Andrew of Greece, and at Tatoi, 'a delicious day'.

On the way home to England they stopped in Paris, where the recently crowned King and Queen of Norway were made very welcome on their state visit, apart from Queen Maud's carriage being upset. She had been the youngest and prettiest of the Wales sisters. When Norway separated from Sweden, Maud's husband, Prince Charles of Denmark, became King Haakon of an independent Norway. Princess Victoria of Wales wrote to Louisa: 'I . . . did so enjoy going to my little sister who thank God seems quite happy in her new capacity. It did seem strange seeing her crowned!! of all people.'

The English summer season was no anti-climax for Louisa. She was staying with the Waldorf Astors at their palatial seat, Cliveden, on the Thames, when they all motored over to Windsor for the garden party: 'it rained a little but otherwise was rather nice.' Nancy Astor was a true friend to Louisa, sometimes lending her a car, or sitting with her when her fellow-guests were at the races. Angus McDonnell, Louisa's handsome younger son, had first met Nancy, then the lovely Miss Langhorne, in America. 'Girls, you don't have to dress up!' Mrs Langhorne had called to her three desirable daughters, when Angus's cowboy figure hove in sight, paying a call. Later he proposed, but Nancy turned him down. She always remained 'very dear', and was very angry when her faithful swain eventually married.

THE LOSS OF A MILLION IN A MOMENT

The Tragic Explosion on France's Great Warship, the "Iéna,"

at Toulon  March 12, 1907.

Below: the remains of the French battleship *Iéna* as seen from the royal yacht at Toulon.

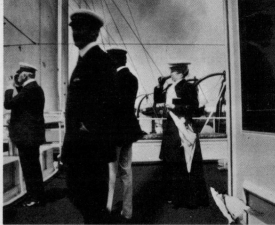

The royal yacht approaches Cartagena.

'From Gib to Toulon: Admiralty Yacht', a sketch made for Louisa by Eduardo de Martino, an eccentric Neapolitan inherited as marine painter by the King from Queen Victoria.

The Queen with her officers and dog; the royal pets went on every trip.

The Spanish fleet escorting the royal yacht
on arrival at Cartagena.

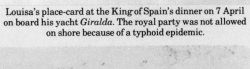

Condesa de Antrim

Louisa's place-card at the King of Spain's dinner on 7 April
on board his yacht *Giralda*. The royal party was not allowed
on shore because of a typhoid epidemic.

Charlotte Knollys with
Louisa on deck.

Maria Christina

Queen Maria Christina, the Dowager Queen of Spain.

King Alfonso of Spain.

Caviar de Sterlet

Tortue claire

Escalopes de Saumon, Sauce Génoise

Cailles à la Diane

Roast Beef à l'Anglaise

Poulardes de Bresse Rôties

Jambon d'York au Madère

Salade à la Jaucourt

Asperges de Lauris, Sauce Mousseline

Timbales à l'Espagnole

Crôutes de Merluches

Bombe Favorite

Carthagène   9 Avril 1907

The dinner given for the King and Dowager Queen of Spain on the *Victoria & Albert*, 9 April.

The officers of the royal yacht: Captain Keppel sits between Princess Victoria and the Queen.

Althorp
S. Neville-Rolfe
Fritz Ponsonby
John H. Ward.
Charlotte Knollys
Howe.
Sidney Greville.
Eduardo de Martino

Lord Howe, Eduardo de Martino,
Sidney Greville, Fritz Ponsonby
and Charles Hardinge.

John Chapple and
Sidney Greville.

Officers in informal mood: Louisa laughed
with them all, and was a great favourite.

Louis Battenberg
Vice Admiral

Malta, 1907.

Prince Louis of Battenberg, Vice-Admiral of the Mediterranean fleet.
The royal yacht called at Malta on the way east.

Lord Althorp,
the Lord Chamberlain.

View from the royal yacht on arrival at the ancient port of Gaeta, between Naples and Anzio.

Menu for the luncheon on board the *Trincatria*.

Group after luncheon on the King of Italy's yacht, *Trincatria*: Princess Victoria, King Victor Emmanuel, King Edward and Queen Alexandra surrounded by their suites and officers of both yachts. Louisa stands second from right.

King Victor Emmanuel of Italy.　　The Queen of Italy.

The *Victoria & Albert* outside Palermo.

Visiting the Whitakers, 26 April, at Palermo. 'A huge house full of horrors and luncheon in the only cold place in the garden', wrote Louisa.

Queen Alexandra on the terrace of the hotel at Palermo.

The King at Palermo.

A visit to the Cathedral.

The King leaving the hotel at Palermo after luncheon, 24 April.

The King of Greece's grandchildren watching
the party leave for Marathon.

Princess Andrew of Greece, daughter of Prince Louis of Battenberg.

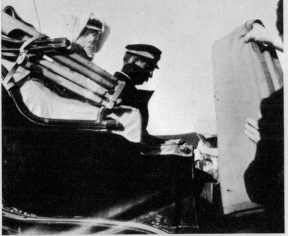
Setting off by motor to Marathon.
The heat was 'grilling', wrote Louisa.

Louisa with Madame Baltaggi,
Princess Andrew's
Lady in Waiting.

Prince and Princess Andrew of Greece.

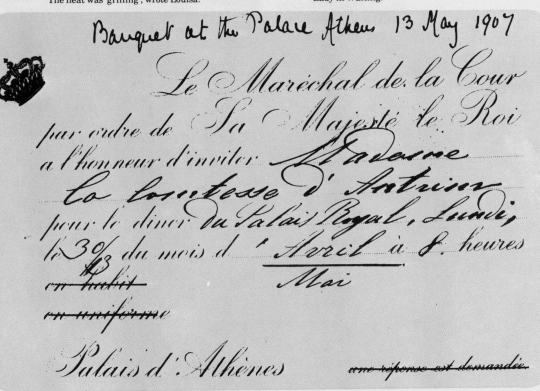
Banquet at the Palace Athens 13 May 1907

Le Maréchal de la Cour
par ordre de Sa Majesté le Roi
a l'honneur d'inviter Madame
la Comtesse d'Antrim
pour le dîner au Palais Royal, Lundi,
le 30 du mois d' Avril à 8 heures
Mai
en habit
en uniforme

Palais d'Athènes   une réponse est demandée

Invitation to a banquet at the Palace, Athens.

Local inhabitants at Marathon.

The Greek Princes at Tatoi.

Prince Nicholas.

The Queen with Captain Keppel.

Luncheon at Tatoi, the royal villa outside Athens:
a relief from the sweltering heat of the Palace.

The Queen and King George at Tatoi.

The royal yacht outside Corfu, by Eduardo de Martino.

The King of Greece's villa, Mon Repos, at Corfu.

After tea at Mon Repos, 4 May.

The view from the walls of Mon Repos.

Louisa walking in the garden.

Tea party, Mon Repos.

Menu du 3 Mai 1907
Dejeuner
Zakouska
Poissons frits
Pommes de terre
Petits Poulets au petits pois
Tornedos à la Parisienne

Mousse au fraises

Fruits et Dessert

Luncheon at Mon Repos May 18·07

Menu for luncheon, Mon Repos.

Pozzuoli. The yacht took shelter here after three days of 'horrid' swell. Even Queen Alexandra, an excellent sailor, decided to continue the trip by land.

Lord Howe and the Queen
in Florence, 24 May.

Smoke rising from Stromboli.

Another royal upset – Queen Maud of Norway's carriage is overturned during a state visit to Paris
at the end of May. Louisa and Queen Alexandra had joined her there on the way home.

A summer houseparty at Cliveden in June.

Early morning ride.

Nancy Astor. Louisa's younger son, Angus, had met her in America before her marriage and had hoped to marry her himself, but the family remained close friends.

William Waldorf Astor with his children.

The river summer house at Cliveden.

Louisa talking to her host, William Waldorf Astor. Nancy Astor is second from the left.

PALACES AND KINGS

ASSASSINATION OF THE
KING OF PORTUGAL.
TO DENMARK, SWEDEN AND
NORWAY WITH THE QUEEN.
THE EMPEROR AT REVAL.
1908

On the last day of January a royal telegram arrived for Louisa in the inconvenient way that royal telegrams did. 'I got a sudden summons to go to Norway with the Queen wh: was a bit embarrassing – however I suppose I can be ready.' Three days later some truly 'awful news' shocked Louisa to the core. King Carlos I of Portugal and his son the Crown Prince had been shot dead on 1 February by terrorists as the family entered Lisbon's famous Black Horse Square in an open carriage. Queen Amélie threw her bouquet at the King's killer – the only weapon she had – and herself in front of her younger son Manoel. 'It haunts one', wrote Louisa, 'to think of that poor Queen who escaped by a miracle.' The world press applauded her heroism, and her son did indeed live to reign as Manoel II – but for less than three years. Portugal became a republic in October 1910 and Manoel an exile in England. In vain the anguished 'Blue Monkey', Louis de Soveral, implored King Edward to support the tottering House of Braganza with warships. Louisa attended the Requiem Mass held for the victims. The presence of King Edward was sharply criticized by Protestant zealots. The Protestants of Glenarm held their peace.

On 20 April, Louisa was ready for the Scandinavian trip, though her wardrobe seems to have been hastily rejigged by her maid Bodley. 'Periwinkle muslin done up – 4 days, black net instead lace – 6 days, grey satin white linen skirt – lengthened.' Bodley also ran up a new lilac dressing-gown, some little hair capes and knickerbockers. In a fortnight they were to visit the Courts of all three Scandinavian countries where the Royal family had relatives. Louisa's diary, not surprisingly, was to register exhaustion: 'to bed immediately after dinner – for wh: we were thankful' 'very delicious to get to bed'.

Louisa commented on a 'cold snowy ugly landscape' all the way to Copenhagen, but their reception at the station made up for nature's bleakness. There was 'a great gathering', wrote Louisa; what Ponsonby called 'a mob of Princes and Princesses'. Her first act next day was to buy goloshes. The banquet at the Palace was 'really very well done', though no doubt Louisa, like Fritz, thought King Frederick was speaking Danish when he gallantly welcomed them in English. After seeing all the palaces and museums, they dined on their last day at Count Raben's – 'very pretty though spoilt by singers at the entrance to the room'. (It was meant to be a concert.)

Stockholm on the twenty-sixth. Louisa was staggered by the magnificence of the art treasures at the Palace. Well she might be, since Napoleon's marshal, Prince Bernadotte, later King of Sweden, had scoured Europe for them. The Palace staircase was lined with soldiers dressed up as Napoleon's Old Guard. Two days later they were in Christiania (Oslo). The informality of a visit to King Haakon's 'little country home' at Bygdø captivated Louisa. Two things, however, were less than pleasing to King Edward: the journalists who photographed the royal party, uninvited, to the great disadvantage, incidentally, of Charlotte Knollys' hideous 'Viking' hat; and the democratic type of monarchy that King Haakon wished to establish. Fritz, probably deputed by his royal master, warned Queen Maud that they would destroy the royal *mystique* if they travelled on the Norwegian tramways.

Afterwards the Household called it the 'Hennessey Trip' because they all returned with three stars.

The next cruise, to Reval (Tallin) in Russia, via the Kiel Canal in Germany, was quite different from the Scandinavian trip. No mere pleasure cruise, this. At Reval the British King and Russian Emperor were to achieve what Philip Magnus, in his *King Edward the Seventh*, calls 'a historic meeting'. One reason stood out for this meeting: the *Weltpolitik* – foreign policy on a world scale – as practised by the Kaiser. He had several times met the Tsar and always tended to patronize him. Since a pact already existed between Britain and Russia, it only remained for Uncle Bertie to help Nicky see the pact as part of a Triple Entente: France, Britain, Russia.

The North Sea treated the *Victoria & Albert* rather as the Kaiser would have liked to treat Nicky – rough. Queen Alexandra was hurled into a corner of the saloon. Picking herself up from a pile of broken tea-cups and biscuits, she burst out laughing. Louisa sat in a deck-house, 'not quite comfortable'. On 7 June they steamed through the Kiel Canal. Prince Henry of Prussia, the Kaiser's son, came on board. It was dark. Gradually Ponsonby became aware of rank upon rank of soldiers, 'a most impressive sight'. Louisa, more perceptive, described the German fleet as 'very large & formidable, saluting as the yacht passed'.

The Baltic was 'beautifully calm' and the two days in quaint, pretty Reval were 'most successful'. The Tsar and Tsarina insisted on visiting the King and Queen first, which, though contrary to protocol, signified a nephew's respect for an uncle. On the first day they all dined on board the Tsar's supremely elegant yacht *Standart*, with its polished masts, white funnels, gilded prow and snowy awnings. Louisa sat next evening between the two key Russians, Foreign Minister Isvolsky and Prime Minister Stolypin, 'very nice for me'. And very nice for them too. Peter Stolypin was to send some photographs later that year to 'la charmante' Countess. This 'grave, splendid-looking man with a long grey beard', as Ponsonby wrote, was the dynamo who might have solved the problem of Russia's landless peasantry. But the terrorists were to get him three years later in Kiev. In Reval, however, security was strict. No landings, of course. And it was proposed to carry out a body-search of the ladies of the Reval Choral Society before their barge anchored within sound of the *Victoria & Albert*. According to Ponsonby, he prevented this excess, and they sang their 'weird Russian songs' unmolested.

The British Ambassador, Sir Arthur Nicolson, coached King Edward in Russia's needs and difficulties. Nicolson wondered how Stolypin and Isvolsky would get on together at Reval. They would require delicate handling. Perhaps Louisa's *placement* at the dinner between the prickly couple was Nicolson's brilliant idea. No one could have been more tactful and discreet than she. Afterwards, wrote Nicolson's son Harold in his *Lord Carnock*, Stolypin and Isvolsky agreed 'that their British visitors had shown infinite discretion', not asking awkward questions. Indeed the First Sea Lord, 'Jackie' Fisher, had spent his time dancing the hornpipe and waltzing with his adored Grand Duchess Olga. The Kaiser none the less suspected British 'machinations' and was stirred by Reval to new suspicions of 'encirclement.'

A calm return journey except for the Kaiser's Kiel – 'arriving at Kiel we ran into a thunder storm'.

King Carlos I of Portugal. His assassination on 1 February 1908 horrified Louisa and sent a shudder through royal circles.

Crown Prince Luiz; he was shot at the same time as his father.

ILS SONT EN PAIX!
Le Seigneur ne séparera pas dans la gloire ceux qu'il a réunis dans la souffrance.

Memorial card from Queen Amélie, September 1909.

Queen Amélie, hailed by the press as a heroine for her bravery during the attack.

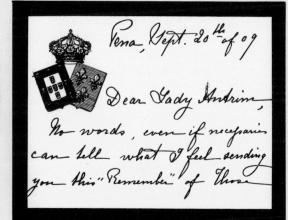

Pena, Sept. 20th of 09

Dear Lady Antrim,

No words, even if necessary can tell what I feel sending you this "Remember" of those

you knew so well!

Remember them, dear Lady Antrim, and remember

Yours most affectionately

Amélie,

Queen Amélie's letter to Louisa enclosed with the memorial card. They had become friends at Windsor in 1904.

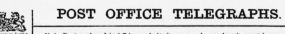

POST OFFICE TELEGRAPHS.

Telegram to Louisa from the widowed Queen after the assassination.

First stop on the royal tour of Scandinavia: the Amalienborg Palace, Copenhagen.

Crown Prince Christian of Denmark and his family.

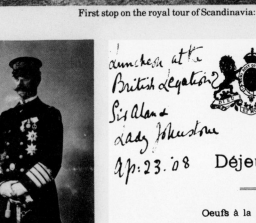

King Frederick of Denmark, Queen Alexandra's elder brother. Her father had died in 1906, aged eighty-nine.

Luncheon at the British Legation Sir Alan & Lady Johnstone Ap: 23.08

Déjeuner

Oeufs à la Parisienne

Filets de Soles froid à la Maintenon

Suprême de Dindonneau Forestière

Noisettes de Presalé à la Marigny

Pommes de Terre

Cailles rôties au Suc d'Ananas

Asperges verte Sauce Mousseuse

Calvilles Alexandra

Gâteaux

du 23 Avril   Légation Britannique

Luncheon at the British Legation;
'hot and long as all such occasions', wrote Louisa.

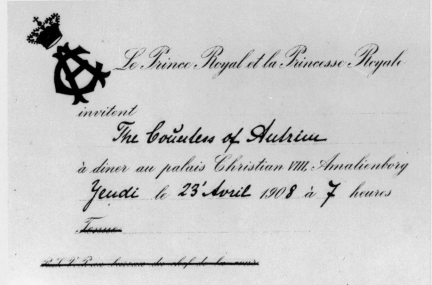

Le Prince Royal et la Princesse Royale

invitent

The Countess of Antrim

à diner au palais Christian VIII. Amalienborg

Jeudi le 23 Avril 1908 à 7 heures

Banquet at the Christian VIII Palace. 'We got to bed by 10.30', wrote Louisa thankfully.
King Frederick made a speech in 'English' which none could understand.

Banquet at the 'huge and beautiful' palace, Stockholm. The English were dazzled by the Sèvres porcelain and splendid French furniture collected by Bernadotte.

Crown Prince Gustaf Adolf and Crown Princess Margaret (daughter of the Duke of Connaught).

The King and Queen of Sweden.

King Gustaf of Sweden.
He gave this photograph to Louisa.

Le 26 Avril 1908.

Diner

Consommé printanière
Rissoles de homard à l'Italienne
Bouchées de soles à la Parisienne
Filet de bœuf aux primeurs
Pâté de foie gras en belle vue
Sorbet dame blanche
Poulardes rôties. Salade Lorette
Tomates à la Reynière
Bombe à la Napolitaine. Friandises
Pailles au parmesan
Fruits
Dessert

The King of Sweden's banquet. 'Magnificent plate, china etc.', noted Louisa, 'but rooms afterwards too small for the company (220 people) . . . very delicious to get to bed'.

PROGRAMME

MONDAY THE 27th OF APRIL 1908.

OUVERTURE TO THE OPERA RIENZI BY R. WAGNER.
CONDUCTOR: *CONRAD NORDQVIST.*

SECOND AND THIRD ACTS OF

OTHELLO

OPERA IN 4 ACTS BY ARRIGO BOITO. MUSIC BY GIUSEPPE VERDI.

CONDUCTOR: *ARMAS JÄRNEFELT.*

OTHELLO, Moor, Venetian General . . . . *Modest Menzinsky*
JAGO, Ensign . . . . *John Forsell*
CASSIO, Lieutenant in the life Guards . . . . . . *Sven Nyblom*
RODRIGO, Venetian Nobleman. . . . . *Barthold Schweback*
LODOVICO, Ambassador to the Republic of Venice *Åke Wallgren*
MONTANO, Previous to Othello, Governor of
Cyprus . . . . *Jean Grafström*
A. HERALD . . . . *Thor Mandahl*
DESDEMONA, Othello's wife. . . . . *Mrs Lykseth-Schjerven*
EMILIA, Jagos wife . . . . *Mrs Clausen*

Noblemen, Noblewomen, Soldiers, Othellos and Desdemonas Pages.

Between the Acts songs will be sung in the Vestibule by
"PAR BRICOLES" CHOIR.

"SPRING SONG" . . . . *Prince Gustaf*
"ORPHEUS SONG". . . . . *O. Lindblad*
"HEAR US, SVEA". . . . . *G. Wennerberg*

Gala Opera at Stockholm.
The royal party went straight from there to catch a train to Norway.

Prince William
of Sweden.

The Crown Princess
and her sister-in-law.

HORSE SHOW
STOCKHOLM

PROGRAMME

APRIL 26TH 1908

School-riding
by winners of 1st & 2nd prize

Jeu de Rose

Military Quadrille

Quadrille
ridden by four officers in 17th century
uniform

Jumping competition.

A display by the famous Swedish cavalry. To Louisa's dismay the
English visitors were whisked off to this the moment they arrived.

Arrival of the royal party
by state coach at Christiania (Oslo).

Kristiania. Slottet med Svanedammen.

The Palace, Christiania. Fritz Ponsonby reported it very large and uncomfortable,
but Louisa admired 'the splendid setting'. There was a grand banquet here on their first evening.

King Haakon and Queen Maud (Queen Alexandra's daughter)
with their son Olav. Haakon had been elected King in 1905.
King Edward found his ideas on ruling alarmingly democratic.

NATIONALTHEATRETS

GALAFORESTILLING

I ANLEDNING AF

DD. MM.

KONG EDWARD

OG

DRONNING ALEXANDRA

AF ENGLANDS

BESØG

DEN 29. APRIL 1908

*

'"Mary Stuart in Scotland", a Historical Drama in 5 Acts',
performed by the Norwegian National Theatre company.

Expedition to Voxenkollen, a popular ski resort.
King Edward was irritated by his son-in-law's informal habit of using standard trains.

An enjoyable respite from the city. Louisa (veiled) beside King Edward,
Charlotte Knollys in her 'Viking' hat, Fritz Ponsonby in tweeds in the back row.

PROGRAM
1STE MAI 1908

KOMZAK:
   Vindolona Marsch.

MAILART:
   Fantasie af Opr. „Villars Dragoner".

CREMIEUX:
   Quand l'amour meurt.

EDV. GRIEG:
   Intermezzo af „Sigurd Jorsalfar".

STRAUSS:
   Walzerträume.

OLE BULL:
   Sæterjentens Søndag.

DONIZETTI:
   Fantasie af Opr. „Regimentets Datter".

OSCAR BORG:
   Nordpol-Marsch.

Programme of music for the last event before leaving for England.
'A sad parting for poor Queen Maud', wrote Louisa.

A walk through the woods at Bygdø to King Haakon's tiny
Victoria Cottage, by the sea. 'Too pretty for words', wrote Louisa.

Princess Victoria and
her sister, Queen Maud, on skis.

The party gathers outside King Haakon's country villa at Bygdø;
King Edward rests by the door.

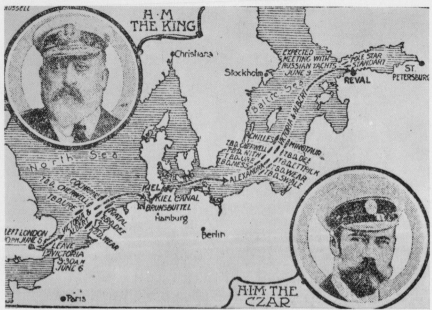

King Edward's journey to meet the Tsar at Reval, June 1908. The visit caused protest in Parliament, which had been horrified by the massacre at the Winter Palace and the Tsar's dismissal of the Duma.

The royal yacht *Victoria & Albert*.

Part of the magnificent escort laid on for the trip.

The Queen and some of her suite on board.

The King and Queen on the royal yacht.

First day on board. Lord Errington (Hardinge's secretary), Sir Arthur Nicolson (British Ambassador to Russia),
Sir Charles Hardinge (Permanent Under Secretary for Foreign Affairs), and the Queen. The picture was taken by a special 'water-lens' camera.

Railway bridge over the Kiel Canal. The party was relieved to reach calm water here after two days of violent 'bucketing' on the North Sea.

The Kiel Canal. At one time the Kaiser had hoped to make it a German equivalent of Cowes, but without success.

Prince Henry, the Kaiser's brother, receiving the King at Kiel.

The German fleet saluting at Kiel.

Prince and Princess Henry's launch, Kiel Harbour.

German torpedo boats escorting the royal yacht out of Kiel Harbour.

The German fleet at Kiel. 'Very large and formidable', noted Louisa.

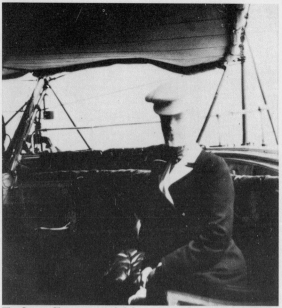

The Queen. She never minded the tossing and turning of rough seas.

The Queen with her dogs.

Mac and Caesar, royal dogs.
Her pets accompanied the Queen whenever possible.

'Jackie' Fisher,
the First Sea Lord, taking
a stroll round the yacht.

Louisa in white yachting hat and coat.

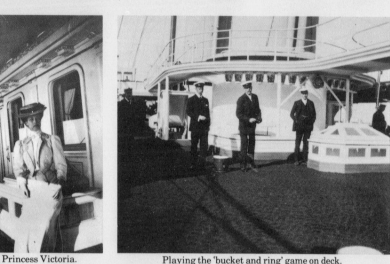

Princess Victoria.

Playing the 'bucket and ring' game on deck.

More games at sea:
Fritz Ponsonby and Lord Hamilton compete.

Group on the royal yacht. Front row, l. to r., Lord Howe, Sir Charles Hardinge, the Queen, the King,
Louisa, Charlotte Knollys, Sir John Fisher, Sir Arthur Nicolson, Eduardo de Martino. Fritz Ponsonby holds Mac.

Lord Howe, Lord Fisher,
Lord Carnock and Lord Hamilton.

The 'Chevalier' de Martino
making a sketch. The King
took him on every trip.

Sir Charles Hardinge, Lord Hamilton, Sir Arthur Nicolson
and General Brocklehurst.

The King's Marine Band.

Reval, 9 June. The Russian fleet was noticeably absent; most of it had been sunk by the Japanese in 1905.

The old Russian town of Reval (now Tallin).

The Tsar arriving with the Tsarina and their family; he insisted on making the first call. On the left is the Russian Prime Minister, Peter Stolypin.

Sir Arthur Nicolson dressed for the Tsar's visit. The King disapproved of his choice of decorations.

Louisa with Captain Stanley. The weather at Reval was perfect, and Louisa made full use of her camera.

The Tsar's yacht *Standart*, the largest and grandest of all the royal yachts.

Michael
Olga
Nicolas
Peter Oldenburg
Peter St. typme
Maria

DÉJEUNER

DU 27 MAI 1908.

Potages | Princesse

Consommé à la Toulouse

Petits pâtés

Homard au Champagne, froid

Roulettes de Gélinottes truffées

en Vol-au-vent

Canards Nantais aux petits pois

Pêches à la Vanille et Purée de fraises glacée

Fromages

Dessert.

The King and Queen setting off by launch
for the reception on the *Standart*.

The Tsarina Alexandra. She
lived in an agony of worry over
her son's health, and was found
weeping alone at one moment
during the King's visit.

Marie Alexandra

The Dowager Empress Marie and her sister, Queen Alexandra.
They were very close, and shared a villa in Denmark.

Luncheon on the Dowager Empress's yacht,
Polar Star, on 9 June. The thirteen-day
difference in dates arises from the use on the
menus and programmes of the Russian
calendar.

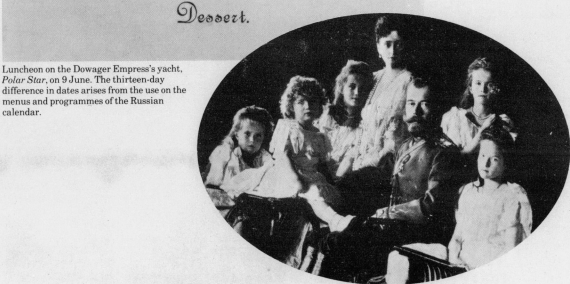

The Tsar and Tsarina
with their children.

The King saluting his niece, the Tsarina, on board the *Standart*. He wore the uniform of the Kiev Dragoons.

The *Standart*. The bow was encrusted with gold leaf.

The King and Queen arriving for the reception on the *Standart*.

The Tsarevitch, Alexis, aged not quite four. He suffered from haemophilia.

The letter from Peter Stolypin enclosing photographs for 'the charming Lady Antrim'. Stolypin was assassinated in 1911.

King Edward with the Tsar's daughters. They were all killed in 1918.

On the Tsar's yacht. The Tsar talks to Sir John Fisher, left; King Edward is on the right. The meeting was a great success.

Menu for the luncheon on the *Standart*, with signatures of the Tsar's children.

The Tsar's five daughters.

РЕВЕЛЬСКОЕ МУЗЫКАЛЬНОЕ ОБЩЕСТВО

„ГУСЛИ“

состоящее под покровительством

ЕГО ИМПЕРАТОРСКАГО ВЫСОЧЕСТВА

Великаго Князя

ВЛАДИМИРА АЛЕКСАНДРОВИЧА.

26 Мая 1908 г.

The Reval Musical Society's programme.
They sang alongside the royal yachts, accompanied by balalaikas.
The first song was 'Let the Tsar Live For Ever'.

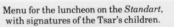

Luncheon on the *Standart* on the final day, 10 June.

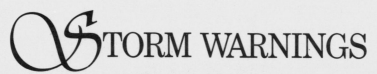

Storm Warnings

STATE VISIT TO BERLIN.
VOTES FOR WOMEN.
LAST CRUISE WITH THE KING.
1909

No one had a livelier sense of duty than King Edward, at least where diplomacy was concerned. He bowed to his Cabinet's decision that a state visit to the German capital was essential, if the clouds caused by Reval were to be dispersed. The Kaiser had been pressing him to come for years. Edward hated the prospect, especially when Berlin was ice-bound and Biarritz beckoning. As for Alix, she had always loathed the Germans, ever since the Kaiser's grandfather, impelled by Bismarck, had seized Schleswig-Holstein from its Danish claimants.

The State Visit to Berlin, 9-12 February, turned out to be something of a *danse macabre*. Despite the Kaiser's passion for organization, several things were to go ludicrously wrong, while their Majesties were both 'seedy', the King with his usual bronchial trouble, the Queen recovering from severe influenza. Alexandra's natural resilience, however, carried her through the first stage – a very bumpy train journey. When a footman upset a dish of quails, one landing on her *toupée*, she delighted all present by saying as she disentangled it, 'I shall arrive in Berlin *coiffée de cailles*'.

A *faux pas* occurred on the arrival platform itself. Edward stepped out from Alexandra's compartment instead of his own, so that the enormous concourse of stout German royalties had to canter up the platform to receive him. Louisa noted only 'the greatest pomp and ceremonial', the 'magnificent' drive through the town from the station to the Schloss and the 'troops everywhere' among the crowds.

On this first day Louisa enjoyed 'a great reception at the Schloss', 'a big household luncheon' and 'a very pleasant banquet in the Weisse Saal', sitting between the German Chancellor Prince von Bülow and the British Ambassador. (Things cannot have been 'very pleasant' for Bülow, since the Kaiser was preparing to dismiss him.) But most of all Louisa enjoyed 'a good sleep' between lunch and dinner, 'for I was very tired'.

Next day was to produce the King's best moment, followed immediately by his worst. In the Rathaus he charmed the dignified city fathers off their perches; a success that was by no means hampered by the absence of his nephew. But at the British Embassy luncheon-party disaster struck. Strapped into a tight Prussian uniform, he had eaten copiously and was smoking one of his huge cigars as he talked to Her Serene Highness the Princess of Pless, when he choked and fainted. Her *Serene* Highness – more irony – thought, 'My God, he is dying', and struggled in vain to undo the buttons of his collar. However, Queen Alexandra succeeded, the King came round, and his physician Sir James Reid issued a 'No cause for alarm' statement on the King's instructions. Nevertheless death had not been far off. In the macabre spirit of this visit they inspected a medical institute that very afternoon. 'We did not stay long', noted Louisa, who was enjoying the lantern slides.

Louisa found the state ball in the evening 'really a most beautiful sight'. Not so Daisy Pless. She has described in her memoirs the bizarre spectacle of an officer cadre, the most modern in the world, forbidden by antiquated protocol to dance anything but old-fashioned minuets, gavottes and quadrilles. Daisy made no bones about her contempt for German arrangements compared with British. The Kaiser had once suggested she should turn Kiel into a Germanic

Cowes. What a hope, with men drinking nothing but beer, and women a despised race. (The ladies, including Daisy, had not been allowed to ride in the procession on the ninth.)

On the eleventh the weather was too bitter to visit Potsdam as planned. Instead they walked all through the imperial stables – 330 beautiful horses with carriages to match. The day ended with a gala performance of the Kaiser's own ballet, *Sardanapal*. King Edward woke up during the last scene when the Babylonian monarch lights his own funeral pyre, imagining the theatre to be on fire and calling for the fire-engines.

Punch's Almanack for 1909 showed that there were stresses and strains on the domestic front also. The women's movement battled its way forward, and daughters of Court ladies were apt to declare themselves followers of Mrs Pankhurst. Louisa's Sybil was sent to prison for militancy, and the health of Lady Lytton's Constance was ruined by forced feeding. On the other side, Cabinet ministers like H.H. Asquith and Winston Churchill were physically threatened. But for his wife, Churchill would have been toppled off a railway-platform. (Mary Soames, *Clementine Churchill*, 1979.) One irate and ribald peer, Lord Carson, ordered his butler to bring out a kettle and dribble water on the pavement beneath a suffragette who had chained herself to the railings in Parliament Square, thus driving the poor lady home. Lloyd George's 'People's Budget' was presented at the end of April. The King privately denounced it as class war. He and his family, however, were by now once more cruising in the Mediterranean.

Short-tempered because far from well, Edward was not always easy to deal with. At Malta there was a contretemps in which his brother Arthur of Connaught became involved, over the fleet's being in Greek waters instead of in the Mediterranean to greet him. Louisa tactfully played down this affair: 'A lovely day', she wrote, 'the Duke & Dss of Connaught came on board – the fleet had already sailed for Lemnos – wh: was rather a pity'. Louisa was herself the silent witness of an amusing scene on the slopes of Mount Vesuvius. 'Naples. May 1. We started at 11 to go up Vesuvius & had a long & interesting expedition – but we could not manage to get up to the Crater.' In reality the expedition was much too 'long' for the King and not 'interesting' enough. He remained with the little train they had arrived in, while the Queen, her sister Marie and some of the Household set off for the top. Louisa soon dropped out. Alexandra, Marie and Ponsonby, however, plunged ahead. The King meanwhile got bored with waiting. Whistle, whistle, whistle from the engine. The three lost their nerve and returned without seeing the crater, Ponsonby on the slowest donkey bearing the full brunt of H.M.'s wrath.

Other expeditions were 'delicious': Palermo, 'a great day of sight-seeing'; Baia with the camera-mad King of Italy, everyone snapping and saluting; Athens, 'I got some stuff for making up'; Corfu, 'welcome letters & 4 days papers'; Venice, 'gondolas . . . serenade . . . to a lace shop & eventually ruined myself over a lace gown'. On the grilling train home they 'dripped all thro' the journey'.

Home meant the safe birth of a child at last to Ducie and Peg; and it meant Bill. 'I found Bill well but just as lame as ever, poor thing', wrote Louisa. Poor King also: Louisa was home from her last cruise with Edward VII.

Programme for the state visit to Berlin, February 1909.

The royal yacht *Alexandra*, which took the party to Calais.

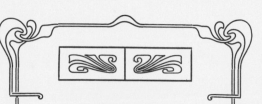

Journey to

BERLIN and Back

OF

THEIR MAJESTIES

The King and Queen

AND THEIR SUITE.

Leaving LONDON on
Monday, February 8th, 1909.

First page of the programme for the journey.

Uncle and nephew in the procession through Berlin.
Louisa noted 'huge crowds and troops everywhere'.

a list of Suite in attendance

WINDSOR CASTLE.

Precedence of the Suite (Berlin).
----

(1). Earl of Crewe.

(Lord Privy Seal and Secretary of
State for the Colonies).

(2). Viscount Althorp. (Lord Chamberlain).

(3). Earl Howe. (Lord Chamberlain to
The Queen).

(4). Earl Granville. (Lord in Waiting to
The King).

(5). Field Marshal Lord Grenfell.

(Gold Stick in Waiting and
representing the Army).

(6). The Right Hon: Sir Charles Hardinge.

(Permanent Under Secretary of State
representing the Foreign Office).

(7). Admiral Sir Day Bosanquet.

(Representing the Navy and appointed
Governor of South Australia).

(over).

Precedence list for the King's suite:
an all-important matter in the Kaiser's Court.

Berlin

Königl. Schloss

The Kaiser's vast palace. The stairs were lined with officers
in the uniform of Frederick the Great for the King's reception.

Invitation to Louisa to the royal banquet
on the first evening.

Two of the Kaiser's six sons,
Prince Joachim (above) and
Prince Oskar (below).

Music programme for the banquet: a tactful blend
of English and Scottish songs and German marches.

The Kaiser making his welcoming speech at the banquet.
Louisa sat at the 'gala table' next to the Chancellor, Prince von Bülow.

Déjeuner du 10. Février

Caviar au Citron

Filets de Soles à la Tartare

Selle de Pré-salés Bouquetiere

Sûpreme de Gélinottes aux Truffes

Timbale de Foie gras de Strassbourg

Salade Lorette

Bombe Grande Duchesse

Macédoine de Fruits

Petits Gateaux

Pailles au Parmesan

Dessert

The Empress with the Queen,
leaving the Kaiser Friedrich Museum.

Menu for the luncheon at the British Embassy which proved nearly
fatal for the King. He had a severe fit of choking and fainted.

Auf Allerhöchsten Befehl

Jhrer Kaiserlichen und Königlichen Majestäten

beehrt sich der unterzeichnete Ober-Hof-und Haus-Marschall

Countess of Antrim

zum Ball am 10ten Februar 1909 um 8¾ Uhr

im Königlichen Schlosse zu Berlin

einzuladen

Ueber Anzug, An-u. Abfahrt pp.
in der beifolgenden Anlage das Nähere.

The ball ('a most beautiful sight') at the Kaiser's palace. The dances were old-fashioned minuets,
though the Kaiser's children had tried in vain to introduce the two-step.

King Edward talking to the pretty Princess Salm
at the British Embassy luncheon.

Königliche Schauspiele

Sardanapal

Große historische Pantomime
in 3 Akten oder 4 Bildern

unter Anlehnung an das gleichnamige Ballett Paul Taglionis
neu bearbeitet von **Friedrich Delitzsch**

Musikalische Begleitung (unter freier Verwertung historischer
Originalmotive und einzelner Teile der Hertel'schen Partitur)
von **Joseph Schlar.**

Begleitende Dichtung von **Joseph Lauff.**

Gala performance of the ballet *Sardanapal*,
the Kaiser's own production. It had a spectacular ending, when
King Sardanapal sat on all his treasure and set fire to it.

The Reichstag, Berlin.

PRINCE EITEL FRIEDRICH
Might do for the Tsardom

Napoleon the Great followed his con-
quests of various European countries
by placing his relations on their
thrones. If—we say IF—Kaiser
Wilhelm is successful in all the wars
he is waging on the Continent, will
he fix up his stalwart sons in the
same way? We omit England from
the scheme as, if the Germans come
here, William will naturally "bag"
our Imperial sceptre for himself, being
a grandson of Queen Victoria

THE CROWN PRINCE
Future Kaiser and King of Prussia

PRINCE AUGUST WILHELM
Possible Emperor of the French

The Kaiser's three eldest sons, with their prospects considered by a London newspaper of the day.

Souvenir photograph given to Louisa personally by the Kaiser.

The Brandenburg Gate,
fifty years before the Berlin Wall.

Current affairs as seen by *Punch's Almanack*, 1909, including the famous Fisher-Beresford row (how many battleships to keep up with the Kaiser?), House of Lords reform, the suffragette movement and the Kaiser's expansionist ambitions.

CHRISTMAS MORNING

Mr. DICKY BIRD : " Been to a Suffragette Meeting, have you ! My word, you'll expect me to lay the eggs next."

Card from Princess Victoria to Louisa, who had been to a suffragette meeting.

The kind of girl the King would vote for! The beautiful Miss Whitelaw, who had just married his equerry, Johnnie Ward.

"A perfect woman, nobly planned To warn, to comfort & command"

Mr Asquith – not Louisa's favourite politician.

'Votes for women', a contemporary comment.

Mrs Pankhurst appealing to the workers.

Sybil, in the form of a long published article, appealed to a more cultured audience. She went to prison for her 'militant tactics'.

Victoria

Alexandra

Edward R & I.

Marie Feodorovna

King Edward on the *Victoria & Albert*, April 1909. It was to be Louisa's last voyage with him.

The royal yacht in Genoa harbour.

The Dowager Empress Marie of Russia, Queen Alexandra's sister, who was with the party.

The King and Queen watching the shore as the royal yacht leaves Genoa.

Louisa, Sir Rennell Rodd (the British Ambassador in Italy), Countess Heiden, Sidney Greville, Empress Marie, the King.

At Malta – the Duke of Connaught boards the royal yacht.

Group on board. L. to r., Princess Victoria, Fritz Ponsonby, Harry Stonor, Louisa, Sidney Greville.

The Duchess of Connaught in her garden at Valletta. The royal party had luncheon here.

MALTA. PORTA REALE.

Souvenir postcard of Valletta.

Maria Feodorovna

Signed portrait given to Louisa by Empress Marie.

View of Valletta harbour across the bows of the yacht.

Luncheon at Vadala. A group photograph with the Governor and Lady Grant and local dignitaries. Louisa stands, centre, with feather boa.

Tea at a monastery.
The Queen of Italy with the reverend fathers.

The King of Italy, camera in hand, enjoys the view at Baia.

An expedition to Baia, with the King and Queen of Italy.

Luncheon on the Italian royal yacht:
Louisa's place-card.

The launch from the Italian yacht.

Sightseeing at Pompeii, 3 May.

The royal party watching excavations at Pompeii.

Resting after lunch: Princess Victoria,
Sir Rennell Rodd, Louisa, Fritz Ponsonby.

The Queen.

Exploring the ruined forum, Pompeii.

Picnic lunch in the 'ladies' luxurious bath saloon' at Pompeii was followed by a Neapolitan serenade.

Leaving Pompeii. It was the King's last day on the cruise – he left the yacht on 4 May.

Luncheon at Castel del Mare, 2 May. The yacht had attempted to put in at Capri, but to Louisa's disappointment was prevented from doing so by rough weather.

Going up Vesuvius, 1 May. Some of the party continued by donkey while the King waited impatiently to return for lunch.

Louisa and Fritz, hoping in vain to land at Capri.

Prince N. Obolensky.
Olga Heiden.

Harry Stone.
Sidney Gonville

Neapolitan performers (who appeared like magic on every expedition) on the balcony of the Hotel Sorrento.

Countess Heiden and Prince Obolensky watch the dancing. Louisa's later note about the Countess adds 'she died of starvation in the Russian Revolution'.

The *Victoria & Albert* arrives at Venice, 19 May.

First sight of Venice from the royal yacht.

The Queen and Empress Marie on the yacht at Venice.

Louisa much enjoyed 'wandering and shopping' in Venice.

Miss Wilson (daughter of the King's friend, Lady Sarah).

The royal yacht moored opposite the Doge's Palace.

Tea party at the Excelsior Hotel on the Lido; Louisa on the left.

VICEREGAL INDIA

THE TAJ MAHAL TO CALCUTTA.
ELEPHANTS AND TIGERS.
MAHARAJAHS AND PARTIES.
1909-1910

To Louisa's delight and surprise, her brother-in-law the fourth Lord Minto had been appointed Viceroy of India in 1905, only eight months after his retirement as Governor-General of Canada. Minto's predecessor Lord Curzon had resigned after quarrelling with the home government. 'I believe a sigh of relief has gone up all over India', wrote Mary Minto, Louisa's sister. '[Curzon's] has been a reign of terror and every official has been reduced to pulp.'

King Edward was anxious that the new Viceroy – *his* representative – should be received with suitable ceremony. But Curzon welcomed the Mintos in shooting jacket and slippers. On hearing of Minto's appointment he had said, 'Imagine sending to succeed *me* a gentleman who only jumps hedges!' Minto had indeed been a fine Gentleman Rider in youth, known to the sporting world as 'Mr Rolly'. It was always as Rolly that Louisa referred to him in her diary. Some three years after Minto's appointment, Louisa was off to the House of Lords with her sister Mary. 'We heard G.Curzon was going to speak – but he put it off.' When he did speak, it was to attack the new Indian policy, which consisted of the liberal Morley-Minto reforms, together with tough measures against terrorists. Louisa left for India on 30 September 1909, a spirited partisan of the Viceroy. She had done her homework – *India through the Ages, India: Its Administration & Progress* (Strachey), *Handbook of India, India in 1893* – leavened by her usual light reading, *Audrey the Actress* and *Bride of the Mistletoe.*

Her itinerary was Marseilles to Bombay by sea and then by train to join the Viceregal Court at Simla. She found the Red Sea unendurable: 'one lived in a perpetual bath', so that her main occupation of writing letters was 'almost impossible'. It was 'a joy' to be off the boat at Bombay, and again '*such* joy' to be off the train, for two days, at Agra. The Taj Mahal 'in the half light of evening was more than my fancy painted', the Fort 'truly marvellous' and Fatehpur Sikri, Akbar's deserted city, 'thrilling'. It was too hot to go to church, 'wh: made me feel rather a heathen', but not too hot to visit a shop full of lovely embroideries. She reached the Simla heights on 19 October, 'after rather terrifying hair-pin bends'. Mary at once showed her the improvements she had made to 'Peterhof', the Viceregal Lodge where Louisa's fellow Lady in Waiting, Lady Lytton, had been Vicereine thirty years before.

They left Simla on the twenty-fifth for Rajputana; first stop Alwar, where Louisa was 'thrilled' by the Maharajah's elephant stalls. Here among the Indian Princes, Louisa saw the British Raj in all its Viceregal splendour, reflecting as it did the pageantry of the King-Emperor's reign. The Viceregal party were escorted from Jaipur station by what Louisa called 'strange men in most marvellous colouring' – in fact, the Maharajah's troop of famous Nagas, yelling and brandishing swords as they leapt among the horses and white-bearded patriarchs in exotic costumes. The route was lined with elephants and hung with welcoming streamers: 'Oh! this joyful day!' 'Truce to thee Minto!' There was a tiger shoot next day, where three thousand beaters created pandemonium with guns, sword-sticks, tom-toms, trumpets and squibs. 'I was lucky enough to see Rolly shoot a large Tigress', wrote Louisa; Mary adding that it was 'between the eyes' at a hundred yards, a shot of which only a Viceroy was deemed capable.

They rode on elephants up to the deserted citadel of Amber. Stand-ing under their pretty Edwardian parasols on the palace roof, they could see distant ranges still scored with ancient fortified walls. Did they ever think that the Raj itself would one day be as dead as Amber, and the Maharajahs' palaces turned into museums and hotels?

In Udaipur the Maharana – more glorious even than a Maharajah, since he was directly descended from the Sun – gave them a state banquet in his floating palace on Lake Pichola, after Rolly had laid the foundation stone of a Minto Hall. In his speech Rolly praised the Native States for avoiding the 'poison' of disloyalty to the King-Emperor. The illuminations on the island were 'too good to be believed', wrote Louisa; an enchantment of magical palaces and flaming watch-towers reflected in a fairy lake. The Maharana himself could not dine with them – caste forbade it – nor could any servant speak to him without holding a towel over his mouth. He must not be polluted by mortal breath.

All through November the Mintos and Louisa continued their royal progress around India. It was Mary's birthday on the thirteenth; and very nearly her last day. They had stopped in Ahmadabad, a centre of unrest where the 'poison' that Rolly had spoken of in Udaipur was active. A youth threw two white balls like turnips at the Viceroy's carriage. One bounced off into the sand. The other was caught by Mary's *jemadar* and thrown into the sand also. All the eleven other carriages passed safely over what turned out to be two bombs. In Mysore Louisa was to feel sorry for the wild elephants captured through tame decoys in the Keddah. Happily even the most obstreperous tusker could not throw a bomb.

Calcutta was another city where the 'poison' had taken hold. Louisa reported 'a public reception – streets packed but not enthusiastic'. Old Sir Pertab Singh, despite his having been called 'Darkie' in Queen Victoria's Jubilee procession, wanted to beat those 'Bengali Babus'. Nevertheless Louisa spent 'a very happy Christmas' at Barrackpore, near Calcutta, the Viceroy's charming bungalow on the Hoogli river. Here they saw in the garden the Temple of Glory, erected by Rolly's Viceregal ancestor, the first Lord Minto, to celebrate the capture of Mauritius a century before. An equestrian statue of Rolly himself stands today beside the Temple; but the glory is departed. He has been put out to grass along with the other bronze Viceregal figures who in Louisa's day occupied the central *maidan* in Calcutta. Lord Minto is lucky not to be behind a hedge or next to a silo, like Lord Northbrook and Lord Montagu. Only Lord Curzon stands proudly on the front lawn. But Louisa was thinking of the past. She went to see the touching monument to Lady Canning. A gentle Vicereine who loved the Indians in spite of the Mutiny, she died at forty-four through getting out of her carriage to sketch the Hoogli, with its dolphins and burning *ghats* and floating funeral wreaths of marigolds – and its malarial mosquitoes. She died from a bite, and her husband soon after her.

Before Louisa returned to London in the new year she had seen, from Darjeeling, the world's highest mountain at dawn; the world's largest banyan tree at the Botanical Gardens, Calcutta; and the world's biggest Government House, also at Calcutta, built by Wellington's brother the Marquess Wellesley – 'beautifully arranged', wrote Louisa, 'but quite huge'.

The Fort. Agra.

Proposed Programme for Lady Antrim's visit to Agra, 16th to 18th October 1909,

———

October.

16th	4-25 P. M.	Arrive from Bombay, met by Captain Gibbs. Motor to Circuit House and have tea.
„	5 P. M.	Visit the Taj.
17th	8-30 A. M.	Visit the Fort.
„	3 P. M.	Visit Itmat-ud-Daulah's Tomb, and then Sikandra (Akbar's Tomb).
18th	8-30 A. M.	Motor to Fatehpur Sikri, 22 miles, Returning about midday.
		After lunch, if there is time, visit the Taj.
„	4-45 P. M.	Leave Agra.

The Fort, Agra, in Louisa's words 'a truly marvellous place'.

Programme for Louisa's first days in India, spent seeing the sights of Agra.

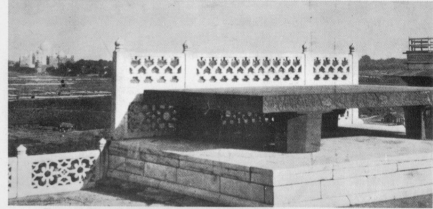
Throne of Jehangir, in Agra Fort. The overthrown Shah Jehan spent his last years here, gazing across the river Jumna at the Taj Mahal, tomb of his beloved wife.

Louisa much admired the delicate pierced marble work of the screens and balconies here, at the Fort.

The Fort, Agra, photographed by Louisa.

The Durbar Hall in the Fort.

The Viceregal Lodge, Simla: 'glorious', wrote Louisa on her arrival on 19 October.

The Earl and Countess of Minto, Viceroy and Vicereine of India.

The Viceregal party left Simla on 25 October.
After a 'beautiful drive' in the carriages they boarded a 'sumptuous train' for Alwar, in Rajputana.

SPRINGTIME ON JAKKO, SIMLA.

Jakko. Louisa visited this beauty spot
during her stay at Simla.

View of the Lansdowne Palace, Alwar. The Vicereine described their stay here as 'the hottest experience we have had in India. The temperature reaches that of the infernal regions.'

His Highness the Maharajah Sewai of Alwar requests the pleasure of Lady Antrim's Company to State Banquet on 26th Octr 1909 at the City Palace at 8. P.m R.S.V.P to the Pres Secy.

Invitation to the City Palace, Alwar.

Street scene, Jaipur.

Soldiers of three generations at Jaipur.

BREAKFAST

Porridge.

Bekti fumée.

Œufs sans gêne.

Œufs et Jambon

Fricasse de Poulet

Curry de Legumes.

BUFFET.

Jambon à l'Aspic.

Faisan rôti.

Galantine de Cannetons.

Terrine de foie-gras.

Langue Écarlate.

Thé — Café.

Chops, Eggs and Omelettes

always available to order.

Breakfast, Franco-Indian style,
at the Lansdowne Palace, Alwar.

The Palace, Jaipur. A grand banquet
was held here for the Viceregal party, with fireworks afterwards.

H.H. Sir Sewai Madho Singh
Bahadur, Maharajah of Jaipur.

Tiger shoot at Jaipur: the iron *machan*, or platform,
from which the ladies viewed the proceedings.

Lord Minto awaits events.

Louisa takes her seat on an elephant.

The luncheon tents.

Triumphant group with 'Rolly's tigress'
and the three thousand beaters needed to outwit her.

Setting off for the visit to Amber:
Louisa and her sister in 'carrying chairs'.

The party admire the view from the Palace roof,
'a glorious stretch of landscape'.

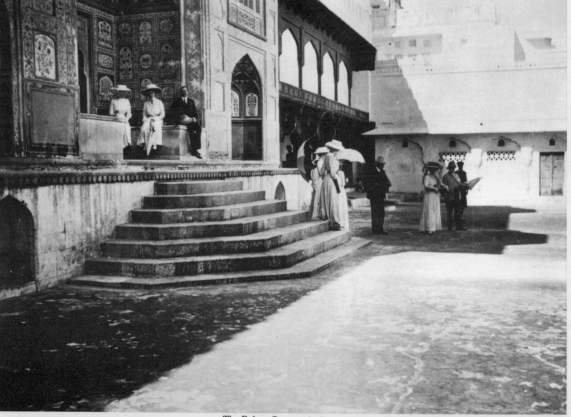

Breakfast was laid in the Durbar Hall, from which
Louisa noted 'a marvellous view – altogether one of the
most impressive sights we have yet seen'.

The Palace Square, Amber.

A quiet moment at Amber. Eileen Elliot, Louisa, Lady Minto
and Joan Howard (the Buzzard's niece, 'Tiger').

Returning from Amber.
Lady Minto leads, Louisa follows.

Udaipur: the market.

The Maharana of Udaipur's floating palace.

The Viceregal party glided over the water in the moonlight to the state banquet at the Palace.

A nobleman in full dress, Udaipur.

The Palace, Udaipur. After dinner the party watched a firework display and Indian dancing.

A splendid array of elephants,
much admired by Louisa.

Part of the reception committee
at Udaipur railway station.

The Maharana's gardens and fountains.

The Viceroy with the Maharana.

H.H. the Maharana
Dhiraja of Udaipur.

Fountains in the Palace gardens.

THE RESIDENCY,
UDAIPUR,
RAJPUTANA.

म॰रा॰फतेहसिंह
ता॰५॰नोवंबर॰सन
१९०२ई॰

The Maharana's signature.

The Viceroy leaving the Palace
after his official visit.

Group at the Begum's garden party, Bhopal.
In the front row are Eileen Elliot, Lady Minto, the Begum, Lord Minto and Louisa.

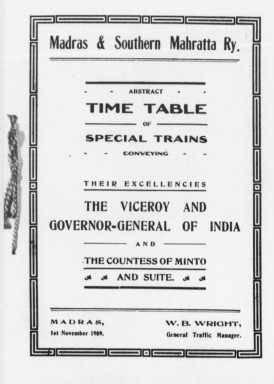

Carefully planned trains laid on for the tour.

Lady Minto with the Maharajah Scindia, 'a real friend,
and one of the most loyal and enlightened Princes in India'.

Watching a sports display at Bhopal: Lord and Lady Minto
with the Begum, her daughter-in-law and her grandsons, 10 November.

Bombay. The party arrived early in the morning
of 17 November to an 'extra cordial' reception.

Lord Minto with the Portuguese Governor of Goa, Monsieur La
Costa. The party spent a day in Goa: 'a bit of Europe planted in
India & speaking of an old and departed glory', wrote Louisa.

Lord Minto at Gaersoppa Falls.

Louisa at Gaersoppa Falls, one
of the highlights of the tour.
They had their first sight of the
Falls by the light of the full
moon, and dined, according to
Mary Minto, 'gazing at this
entrancing scene, which was
occasionally illuminated for our
benefit by rockets, and bundles
of burning hay thrown over to
light up the spray and foam'.

The Falls. The visitors stayed in a bungalow facing a cascade of 830
feet, nearly five times the height of Niagara Falls.

The top of the Falls. They took it in turns to lie on the protruding rock
for a breathtaking view of the full drop.

Group outside the stockade at Keddah Camp, near Mysore, where wild elephants are captured.

The Yuvaraj, brother of the Maharajah of Mysore, and his heir-apparent.

Wild elephants in the jungle.

Elephants in the stockade.

Musicians at the Palace, Mysore.

Watching the elephants from the river bank.

Two tame elephants, with a captive harnessed behind.

Captive elephants being led across the river.

Lady Minto in native dress.

Crossing the river by raft.

Government House, Calcutta.

Miss Howard's carriage joins the procession at a military review.

The household at Government House, Calcutta.

At the military review, Calcutta.

Christine, Lady Minto's *ayah*.

Parasols on the lawn.

'View from my window',
Government House, Calcutta.

New Year's Day, 1910: their Excellencies, visitors and household.

Lady Alexandra Carrington ('Xandra') who travelled back to England with Louisa.

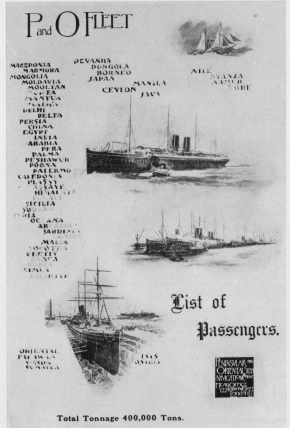

P and O FLEET

MACEDONIA
MARMORA   DEVANHA
MONGOLIA   DONGOLA
MOLDAVIA   BORNEO
MOOLTAN   JAPAN
 VICEA
MANTUA   MANILA
 DELHI   CEYLON   JAVA
 DELTA
PERSIA
 CHINA
EGYPT
INDIA
ARABIA
 PERA
 PALMA
PESHAWUR
POONA
PALERMO
CALEDONIA
PLASSY
 ASSAYE
HIMALAYA
SICILIA
SOUDAN
 OCEANA
ARCADIA
 SARDINIA
 MALTA
SOCOTRA
VECTIS
 BANCA
SIMLA
VALETTE

AILE
AVANZA
NAMUR
KORF

List of Passengers.

ORIENTAL
PALAWAN
SUNDA
SUMATRA

ISIS
OSIRIS

Total Tonnage 400,000 Tons.

Return journey on the *India*,
which left from Bombay on 15 January.

Lady Antrim is to leave Bombay on Saturday for Marseilles, on her way back to England. She has been staying for several weeks in India on a visit to the Viceroy and Lady Minto. Lady Alexandra Carrington is returning home by the same steamer. Lady Antrim will probably go to the Mediterranean in April as lady in waiting on the Queen during their Majesties' intended cruise in the Royal yacht *Victoria and Albert*.

Louisa's photograph of the Suez Canal, 22 January.

THE LAST VOYAGE

CORFU, VENICE AND COMO.
DEATH OF THE KING.
1910

There was no diary for 1910, or after, but Louisa filled up four more albums with pictures. On 14 April she set off on the new royal yacht *Alexandra* for Corfu. Ten days later she stuck in a sheet of signatures and a group photograph that were to mark the future as well as the past. It was to be the last group photograph in which Charlotte Knollys and other old friends in the Queen's suite would stand shoulder to shoulder in the back row. Occasionally Louisa had seemed to resent Charlotte's ugliness – 'Charlotte looking ghastly', she noted once. Charlotte was none the less always given a carefully graded cruise present by Louisa: a statue of St. Bruno (seven shillings and sixpence), as against a St. Francis for Princess Toria (fifteen shillings) and the Queen's St. George (four pounds ten shillings). Looking to the future, the Princess who was to produce the husband for Queen Alexandra's great-granddaughter, Queen Elizabeth II, was sitting in the front row: Princess Andrew of Greece, mother of Prince Philip. From Corfu they went on to Venice, and then to the Royal Victoria Golf Hotel on Lake Como. (Queen Alexandra's idea of golf, wrote Fritz Ponsonby, was to race for the hole as if playing hockey.) They reached Calais on 5 May. Here an ominous letter from the Prince of Wales awaited the Queen.

The King had been at Biarritz with Soveral and Mrs Keppel – 'that horrid Biarritz' as Queen Alexandra called it – from 9 March to 27 April. He had not felt well enough to join the *Alexandra*, as the Queen had hoped. In any case, he needed to be available for England at twenty-four hours' notice. The Liberal Cabinet was locked in a crisis with the House of Lords. The King might be required to dissolve Parliament, perhaps giving an advance guarantee to create five hundred Liberal peers, if the House of Lords continued to veto the government's Finance Bill. He was brought back from the warm south on 27 April.

By 4 May he was wheezing and coughing with bronchitis. It was on this afternoon that the Prince of Wales first warned the party on the *Alexandra*. 'Wrote to Motherdear & Toria to Calais', he entered in his diary, 'where they arrive tomorrow, Wish they were here now.' They joined him on Thursday afternoon, 5 May. 'It was a great shock to them', wrote the Prince, 'to see Papa in this state.' The very next day the end came. Edward received all his family and friends in farewell interviews, his wife magnanimously allowing Mrs Keppel to be among those who called. The last words spoken by this Prince of Pleasure were, 'I am very glad', when they told him that his horse had won at Kempton Park. But his pleasures were not permitted to obscure his political duties. It was as a popular and respected Monarch that he was to be remembered.

The arrangements for his Lying in State at Westminster Hall and his funeral in St. George's Chapel, Windsor, fell largely on the shoulders of Louisa's cousin Fritz Ponsonby and her brother-in-law Pom McDonnell. A fifty-page account of his part in the ceremonies was afterwards written by McDonnell on black-bordered paper from the Office of Works, of which he was head. It began: '*Friday. May 6th. 1910. The King died 11.45 p.m.*' On the ninth, McDonnell saw King George V. 'H.M. was very much affected but very quiet and businesslike ... he said he had lost the best Father and Friend that ever any son possessed.' How helpful Lloyd George had been, added H.M., but 'Winston Churchill quite the reverse', saying that 'he considered a

great change was necessary in the Constitution: whereupon the King remarked that he was averse to violent changes!'

Queen Alexandra received McDonnell on the twelfth. With tears in her eyes, she talked about the suddenness of the King's illness, her complete ignorance of its serious nature until she reached Calais, and 'the providential instinct which warned her to return, in spite of all the arrangements having been made to remain in Venice'. McDonnell said 'it was the finger of God which had beckoned her home! She liked this and repeated it softly to herself twice.' Then she took him into the King's bedroom where he lay in a grey military greatcoat. 'They want to take him away', she said piteously, 'but I can't bear to part with him. Once they hide his face from me everything is gone for ever.' McDonnell left, 'very much broken by the interview', especially by the Queen's conviction that if 'they' had not brought the King home he might have lived.

On the sixteenth, McDonnell was able to meet a hundred press men at Westminster Hall and tell them that all was ready. At 4 o'clock there was a rehearsal, the poor Earl Marshal giving 'an entirely wrong description of what was to be done' and being interrupted by McDonnell. The Lying in State duly began on 17 May, the procession with the coffin leaving Buckingham Palace at 11.30. A 'glorious' service followed, marred only by the loudness of the band that accompanied the choir. The famous hammer-beam roof was too perfect a sounding-board. The royal procession then left, to the strains of Chopin's 'Funeral March', while McDonnell prepared the Hall for the public. Fifty photographers arrived at 3, 'and on the whole behaved very well'. But nothing could be more impressive than the public – 'this mute stream always always passing'. In all a quarter of a million people were to file past the catafalque, headed on the first day by three seamstresses, 'very poorly dressed but very reverent'.

Next day the directions for the funeral were drawn up, King George very efficiently writing everything down, but the Earl Marshal 'looking fogged, and likely', McDonnell thought, 'to make a hash of it'. He did, publishing 'the entire Ceremonial wrong'. It had to be rewritten by four clerks and Dawson, the King's doctor. The King loved the Duke of Norfolk (the Earl Marshal) – 'a charming, honourable, straightforward little Gentleman' but as a man of business impossible. 'I ask you, Pom', H.M. said, 'is it not hard on me?' Pom wrote a memo reforming the system.

There was a visit to the catafalque by the Kaiser. After he had laid a splendid wreath, he and the King clasped hands at the head of the coffin – 'a pretty and dramatic incident'. On the last day, after the doors were shut, four motor cars arrived containing the whole Churchill family. Pom refused them entry. There was a battle royal between Pom, the Keeper of Westminster Hall, and Winston, the Home Secretary. The Keeper won.

The funeral took place at Windsor on 20 May. McDonnell was intensely anxious, but all went well. He saw Mrs Keppel into the Cloister entrance, and tactfully prevented the Empress Marie from throwing her wreath on to the coffin, where it might have caught and stopped the machinery. Louisa, seated in the Chapel among Queen Alexandra's ladies, saw the Master of the Household (Charles Frederick) cast earth upon the coffin, as it slowly sank out of sight.

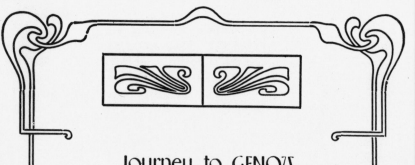

Journey to GENOA

— of —

HER MAJESTY

Queen Alexandra,

H.R.H. PRINCESS VICTORIA,

—— AND SUITE ——

❦

From VICTORIA STATION,

On Thursday, April 14th, 1910.

The last voyage before King Edward's death. From Genoa, the yacht sailed to Corfu.

Old friends on board: Louisa, Lord Howe, Harry Stonor, Princess Nicholas of Greece, the Queen, Sir Arthur Davidson.

The royal yacht at Genoa.

Arrival at Corfu.

Group on the royal yacht, Corfu. Front row, l. to r., the Queen of Greece standing with Princess Andrew's children, the Queen, King George of Greece, Princess Nicholas, Princess Andrew. Louisa and Charlotte Knollys are at the back.

Corfu, viewed from the royal yacht.

The harbour at Corfu.

The Palace, Corfu. The party dined here on 24 April.

Sightseeing at the Achilleion, Corfu.

The King and Queen of Greece in the palace gardens. He was assassinated in 1913.

The Greek royal family.

Corfou. Achilleion. (Villa Imperiale.) Peristyle.

Peristyle of the Achilleion.

A short stop at Venice, and a visit to the Doge's Palace.

Seeing the sights, Venice.

The Piazza S. Marco.

Louisa spent a leisurely hour on a gondola, enjoying the buildings along the Grand Canal.

The hotel on Lake Como; the last sightseeing stop, 4 May.
News of the King's illness reached the Queen at Calais the next day.

The journey home: Louisa.

THE DEATH OF KING EDWARD VII.

KING OF GREAT BRITAIN AND IRELAND AND OF THE DOMINIONS
OVER THE SEAS, DEFENDER OF THE FAITH, AND EMPEROR OF INDIA.

1841   How the News Came   **1910**

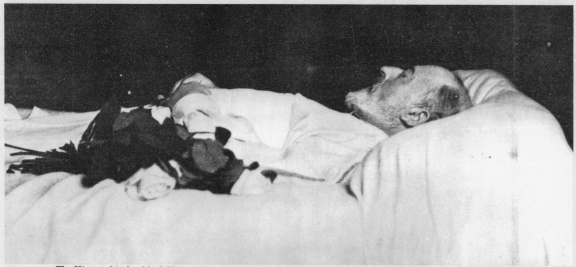

The King on his deathbed. He was sixty-nine. Louisa arrived back in London with the Queen the day before he died.

The King as his friends remembered him, in a homburg hat with his dog Caesar. Caesar followed the gun-carriage at the funeral.

A memorial picture
sent to Louisa by the Queen.

The procession leaving Buckingham Palace, 17 May.

Representatives of the World's Grief.

Some of the foreign representatives

U.S.A.—Represented by ex-President Roosevelt. Montenegro.—Represented by Crown Prince Danilo. Roumania.—Represented by Crown Prince Ferdinand.

Servia.—Represented by Crown Prince Alexander. Egypt.—Represented by Prince Mohamed Ali. Turkey.—Represented by Prince Youssouf Izzeddin Effendi.

Holland.—Represented by Prince Henry of the Netherlands. Italy.—Represented by the Duke of Aosta. Austria.—Represented by Archduke Francis Ferdinand.

Russia.—Represented by Grand Duke Michael Alexandrowitch. France.—Represented by M. Pichon. Japan.—Represented by Prince Sadonaru Fushimi.

Some of the foreign representatives who attended the funeral.

THE FUNERAL
OF
HIS LATE MAJESTY
KING EDWARD VII,
ON
Friday, 20th May, 1910.

—◆—

ORDER
OF
CARRIAGE PROCESSION
FROM
Buckingham Palace to Westminster Hall, and thence to Paddington Station.

Order of the carriage procession to Westminster Hall.

The King of Greece.

The King of Spain.

The Kaiser.

The procession arrives at Westminster Hall. The Queen was in the glass state coach; her ladies, including Louisa, were in a landau.

The Queen driving to Paddington for the funeral in St. George's Chapel, Windsor.

EARL MARSHAL'S OFFICE,

NORFOLK HOUSE,

ST. JAMES'S SQUARE,

S.W.

The Earl Marshal has it in Command to invite

The Countess of Antrim

to assist at the Interment of His late Most Sacred Majesty
of blessed memory in the Royal Chapel of Saint George, at
Windsor, on Friday the 20th instant.

May, 1910.

Gentlemen: Full Dress with Trousers.
Collars and Orders to be worn.
Ladies: Morning Dress.

An *immediate* answer is requested in the enclosed envelope, to enable the
Earl Marshal to forward the necessary ticket.

The royal train steams to Windsor.

Louisa's official summons from the Earl Marshal, the Duke of Norfolk, to the state funeral service.

Half mast at Windsor.

The gun-carriage leaving Windsor station.

The King of the Belgians.

The King of Denmark.

The Kaiser and King George V.

The procession following the gun-carriage.
There had never been so many kings together before.

King Manoel of Portugal.

The King of Norway.

Some of the royal guests in the funeral procession.

THE NEW KING

LOUISA AT KING
GEORGE'S CORONATION.
1911

King George V approached his Coronation burdened by the unsolved problems of his father's reign. Happily the two sides, Liberals and Tories, called a truce for the event. Louisa could not reappear in the glittering gown she had worn at Queen Alexandra's Coronation, for that exquisite confection had been specially designed for the Ladies in Waiting. So she borrowed her sister Lady Minto's robes, and very splendid she looked. She was now seated among the peeresses, all of them ready to lift up their 'white arms' (Louisa had admired them in 1902) in a graceful curve and put on their coronets at the supreme moment of Crowning. There were still plenty of Louisa's old friends in the Abbey, notably Lord Kitchener, carrying 'Curtana', the sword of justice. Nostalgia for the past was an inescapable mood, and Louisa had not failed to attend the service in St. George's, Windsor, for the first anniversary of King Edward's death.

She had written one of her sympathetic letters to Princess Toria. 'Dearest Louisa', replied Toria, 'You told me to call you so, and I *love* doing it. . . . But Goodness! what have you to thank me for. I always love when you come with us.' Though no longer a Lady in Waiting, Louisa's relations with the royal family remained close for the rest of her life. Princess Toria in particular showed that she regarded her as 'one of ourselves'. When Queen Alexandra died in 1925, the unfortunate 'daughter at home' turned to Louisa for support. 'It is a comfort to me to know you are with her this sad Christmas', wrote the Empress Marie to Louisa. She and Toria spent occasional holidays together, having much in common: gardening, bicycling, picking up antiques, reading. 'Dearest Louisa', Toria wrote in 1923, 'I wanted to write myself – & ask if you *cared* to come with me abroad. . . . We have so often been *together* in the early spring that we must *imagine* it to be like old times. . . . I only hope I shall not be a BORE to you.' Toria added that she couldn't get a man to escort them, but – 'I think you & I are quite capable of looking after ourselves don't you.' Later, would Louisa come to Bournemouth? 'I will not bother you at all – you shall do exactly *what* you want – I too can't walk much nor hear & am quite old.' In 1933: 'Do keep up your painting', Toria wrote, 'as really they were lovely sketches you showed me – I only hope I did not talk too much or slander anyone!!' One duty that Louisa had to perform, whether as Lady in Waiting or not, was that of 'banker'. Toria would ask her about subscriptions: 'Would £20 be enough, or £10?' 'Please tell me where to send the two guineas.' Louisa used to say what a 'bad banker' she was on their travels, but Toria maintained she was '*too perfect*' – 'so *dear* and so *understanding* always.' This was the Louisa who cooed 'Mmm, mmm, do go on' under all circumstances – all except one. When her friend the Duke of Argyll died, his valet began telling her about the laying out. 'Mmm, mmm, how dreadful for you.' 'And I had to shave him three times before they buried him, my lady.' Shocked at last into resistance, Louisa exclaimed, 'How perfectly *disgusting!*'.

As the years passed, black-bordered letters and brightly coloured packets of Christmas and Easter cards gathered in Louisa's letter-books: usually views of Windsor or Kensington Palace, or Bagshot where the Duke of Connaught lived, or idealized cottage gardens crammed with old-fashioned flowers. The theme was always the same: remembrance of times past. From Amélie, 1919: 'the happy and for ever gone days.' From Haakon, 1940: 'happy times on the *Victoria & Albert.*' From Beatrice, 1943: 'the older one gets the more one lives in the past.' From Victoria Eugenia, 1944: 'those happy days of my childhood.' From Olga, daughter of the Empress Marie: 'remembrances of the happy past.'

Most of the royal ladies with whom Louisa corresponded were widows, and she herself had become a widow in 1918. The Buzzard slowly ebbed away at Glenarm, first on two sticks, thumping wrathfully to and fro in his grey felt two-gallon hat; then anchored to the dining-room, looking at the lighthouse on Mull, or in the porch, gazing up the Glen. The mobility of his steam cars had increased as his own diminished. His car once bounded out of a side road to disrupt a funeral cortège with hisses and hoots, driving the coffin into the ditch and scattering the mourners like chaff. When his own end came he chose a somewhat pagan burial. (He never seems to have had close relations with the Church. On being asked permission by the villagers to commemorate the late vicar with a plaque, he said: 'Do what you like; dig him up, stuff him if you like.') He himself was buried standing up on the top of Paddy's Hill, under a cromlech looking out to sea. It was rumoured, however that his farm-workers, tiring of their burden and the long climb, tipped him in upside down and facing inland.

As one of Louisa's children put it, she now settled down 'to enjoy the fruits of widowhood', moving to Chelsea Park Gardens next door to her sister Lady Minto. There she would give little luncheons for her royal friends. Hers may have been the initiative, but she was not a snob, says her granddaughter Lady Rose Baring. 'She had what all those Greys have – a sort of other-worldly quality.' In her old age – she lived till April 1949, nearly ninety-four – she was not really as sad and lonely as she sometimes pretended, in deference to royal widows. 'It is so sad to think that *all* the English cousins are gone!', wrote Princess Olga when Louisa was ninety-one. 'I can quite understand that one must feel lonely at 91 – with hardly anyone left to whom you can say "Do you remember?".' True, Louisa had early lost the support of her brother-in-law Pom McDonnell. Writing from the trenches in 1915, he begged her to 'cheer up' his wife Ethel with a letter. But this was beyond even Louisa's sympathetic skill, for Pom was killed a week later.

Her daughter Sybil looked after her, bringing her into the group companionship of Moral Rearmament; the only disadvantage perhaps being that it sometimes made her wonder whether she had been quite fair to Bill, leaving him alone so much. Her little house in Chelsea was burgled four times, so that she lost most of her royal mementoes and complained to her great-grandson, Hector McDonnell, 'Now all I have left is a lock of Bill's hair and Ducie's first tooth.' She was full of sparkle to the last, and loved being asked for stories about far-off days, being essentially one of those curtseying Victorian Ladies in Waiting whom Queen Marie of Roumania described: 'all smiles and with the mellowed voice usual to those who served the great little old lady'. When Princess Toria died in 1935, Louisa copied out the account of her funeral. 'Like figures in a dream', wrote the reporter, of the silent black-clothed mourners with strangely white faces. But, for Louisa, a happy dream.

Queen Victoria's memorial,
unveiled outside Buckingham Palace on 16 May 1911.

Louisa's admission ticket.

Procession to the memorial.

King George V, who unveiled
the memorial to his
grandmother.

The Kaiser, present at the
unveiling ceremony.

Unveiling of the QUEEN VICTORIA MEMORIAL
by His Majesty The King, accompanied by Her
Majesty The Queen, and Their Imperial Majesties
The German Emperor and Empress, on Tuesday,
the 16th May, 1911.

———

HYMN.

f O GOD, our help in ages past,
    Our hope for years to come,
    Our shelter from the stormy blast,
    And our eternal home ;

mf Beneath the shadow of Thy Throne
    Thy Saints have dwelt secure ;
    Sufficient is Thine Arm alone,
    And our defence is sure.

    Before the hills in order stood,
    Or earth received her frame,
cr From everlasting Thou art GOD,
    To endless years the Same.

p A thousand ages in Thy sight
    Are like an evening gone ;
    Short as the watch that ends the night
    Before the rising sun.

    Time, like an ever-rolling stream,
    Bears all its sons away ;
    They fly forgotten, as a dream
    Dies at the opening day.

f O GOD, our help in ages past,
    Our hope for years to come,
    Be Thou our guard while troubles last,
    And our eternal home.   Amen.

Hymn sung at the ceremony.

*The Lord Chamberlain is
commanded by The King to invite*

The Earl & Countess of Antrim

*to the Ceremony of the Unveiling of
The Queen Victoria Memorial
by His Majesty The King accompanied by Her Majesty The Queen
on Tuesday 16th May 1911 at 12 o'clock noon.*

*Levée Dress. Ladies Morning Dress.
An answer is requested addressed to the Lord Chamberlain, St James's Palace.*

Invitation to Louisa and the Buzzard to attend the event.

'All Hail! "This Royal Throne of Kings, This Sceptred Isle"': Byam Shaw's allegory of past monarchs greeting their successor.

Louisa's last signed portrait of Queen Alexandra.

King George V and
Queen Mary, crowned
on 22 June 1911.

Louisa, dressed for the Coronation in robes
made for her sister, Lady Minto, for the last Coronation.

The presentation box to Queen Alexandra from her Household, 7 March 1913,
to commemorate the fiftieth anniversary of her arrival in England.

MAY ALL GO WELL WITH YOU!
MAY LIFE'S SHORT DAY
GLIDE ON PEACEFUL
AND BRIGHT,
WITH NO MORE CLOUDS
THAN MAY GLISTEN IN THE
SUNSHINE, NO MORE RAIN
THAN MAY FORM
A RAINBOW.